D0841257

What they say about THE PASSPORT

*'What Martin Lloyd does not know about crossing
frontiers is probably not worth knowing'*
BBC RADIO 4 'MIDWEEK'

'a lively and thoughtful book'
SUNDAY TELEGRAPH

'a pacey and entertaining history'
HOLIDAY WHICH 'RECOMMENDED READ'

*'Lloyd writes as an eager enthusiast and an expert,
a mix that makes for top entertainment'*
THE GOOD BOOK GUIDE

*'fascinating history
...great rare images of passports from the past'*
LIVING HISTORY

*'a quite simply brilliant book that could be read
in one day – it is that enjoyable'*
EYE SPY

'fine writing in this very interesting book'
CITY TO CITIES

'enthralling... splendid value for such a good read'
JOURNAL OF KENT HISTORY

'a very entertaining and readable book'
BROADLY BOATS

THE PASSPORT

THE HISTORY OF MAN'S MOST
TRAVELLED DOCUMENT

*To Peter
best wishes
Martin Lloyd*

Martin Lloyd

Queen Anne's Fan

This revised and enlarged edition published in 2008 by

Queen Anne's Fan
PO Box 883 • Canterbury • Kent • CT1 3WJ
Reprinted 2009, 2010 (twice), 2011, 2012

© Copyright Martin Lloyd 2003 and 2008
First published by Sutton Publishing in 2003

ISBN 9780 9547 1503 8

A CIP record of this book can be obtained from the British Library.

Set in New Baskerville 11 on 12pt.

Martin Lloyd has recorded THE PASSPORT as a 'talking book'
for the blind, RNIB catalogue no: TB14107

Printed in England

Queen Anne's Fan

CONTENTS

ACKNOWLEDGEMENTS

I thank the following who gave willingly and freely of their time and resources to assist me in writing this book: Peter Bates, (Folkestone), Jonathan Gration (Amsterdam), Margaret Gration (Hawkhurst), John Hunt (Canterbury), Guy G. Van Keer (Brussels), Isabelle Lloyd-Cook (Folkestone), Pete Roberts (Eastry), Valentina Vaselli (Turin).

The excerpt from *The Anglo Saxon Chronicle* is copyright Everyman Publishers PLC, 140a Shaftesbury Avenue, London WC2H 8HD and is reprinted with their permission.

The excerpt from *Horace Walpole's Correspondence with Mary and Agnes Berry and Barbara Cecilia Seton* edited by Lewis and Wallace is copyright Yale University Press and reprinted with their permission.

The excerpts from *Horace Walpole's Correspondence, Vol 20 with Sir Horace Mann* edited by W.S.Lewis, Waren Hunting Smith and George L. Lam (1960) and *Travel in England in the Seventeenth Century* by Joan Parkes (1925) are reprinted by permission of Oxford University Press.

The excerpt from *Elizabeth and Mary Stuart* by F.A. Mumby, Constable, 1914 is reprinted with permission of Constable & Robinson Publishing Ltd.

The excerpt from *The Lithuanian Statute of 1529* is reprinted with permission of Brill N.V. of Leiden.

The excerpts from *Passport Systems: Replies from Governments to the Enquiry on the Application of the Recommendations of the Passport Conference of 1926*, published by the League of Nations 1937 are reproduced with the permission of United Nations Publications.

The excerpt from *The Journal of John Jourdain 1608-1617* edited by W. Foster, Hakluyt Society, 1905 is reproduced by permission of David Higham Associates.

I have tried and failed to find the owners of the copyright in some of the material I have quoted. I would be pleased to insert an acknowledgement in future editions.

I am grateful to the following sources for providing illustrations:

Those on pp. 58, 68, 119, and 171 are from the collection of Guy G. Van Keer.

The illustration on p.128 is Crown Copyright material from *Immigration, Nationality and Passports* (Home Office, 1988) and is reproduced (complete with spelling mistake) with the permission of the Controller of Her Majesty's Stationery Office.

The illustrations on pp. 10 and 137 are from files in the Public Records Office.

All remaining illustrations are from the author's collection.

Martin Lloyd
Canterbury, 2008

1

MURDER AT THE OPERA

The finely dressed passengers alighted from their carriages and fiacres before the Paris Opera, the line of gaslamps lighting the horses' breath as it hung in the crisp winter air. Some of the theatre-goers sought refuge from the chill by waiting inside the vestibule but many stood outside, chattering gaily under the glass awning. They provided a free spectacle of colour and vivacity for the poorer Parisians who thronged the pavements and café terraces of the rue Le Peletier.

There was a feeling of expectancy and excitement in the crowd. It was Thursday 14 January 1858 and all Paris knew that the Emperor Napoleon III and his attractive Spanish wife, the Empress Eugénie, were visiting the Opera that evening.

It was a little after half past eight when there was a stir in the crowd. *'Ils arrivent, ils arrivent.'* In a clatter of hooves the procession turned into the street. First the carriage carrying the court attendants, then the Imperial carriage itself followed by an escort of Imperial Lancers. The crowd surged forward, straining for a view. Unseen in their midst, a man lobbed an object over their heads towards the carriage. A brougham manoeuvring in the street momentarily obstructed the Imperial carriage, obliging it to slow down and at that moment, a metal globe was seen bouncing along the ground towards it. There was a deafening explosion and the street was plunged into darkness as the gas lights of the Opera and the windows of the buildings were shattered. The crowd screamed, the horses reared in terror, scores of people staggered and stumbled away from the carnage.

With remarkable presence of mind, the coachman, Ledoux, whipped up his horses as the escort of Lancers charged forward to surround the carriage. There was a second explosion, maiming one of his horses, and then a third, right beneath the carriage itself. The air was full of deadly shards of flying metal and glass. Those who could, ran in panic. Miraculously, the Emperor and Empress appeared untouched and were hurried into the Opera House by those of the Garde de Paris still able to stand. The question on everybody's mind was, 'who could have perpetrated such a murderous plot?'

The answer was: Count Felice Orsini, but even he could little have imagined the wider repercussions of his attempt. Apart from the hideous cost in human terms – eight people killed and over a hundred injured – his actions had a devastating influence in quite another sphere for the passport that Orsini had used to enter France brought down the British Government of the day and caused the system for issuing passports to be changed forever.

Felice Orsini was an Italian revolutionary, or more precisely, a Piedmontese revolutionary. Italy in the nineteenth century was not yet a unified nation but rather an amalgam of kingdoms and duchies. Its unity was obstructed by the different laws in each and its trade was crippled by a multitude of customs regimes levied in any one of the several currencies in circulation. The administration of Italy was subject to the varying influences of Austria, the Kingdom of Sardinia, the Kingdom of the Two Sicilies and the Papal States.

Orsini was a product of this mish-mash. His involvement in the complex politics of the Italian peninsula and the struggle for its unification was almost inevitable. At the age

Felice Orsini,
1819-1858.

In order to
attempt the
assassination of
Napoleon III
in 1858,
he entered
France by
impersonating
the holder of a
British passport.

of nine he was already accompanying his father, Andrea, on his political excursions against authority and his imprisonment at the age of twenty five for conspiring against the governments of Italy did not divert him from his course. By the time he was thirty five, Orsini was in prison again but this time he was sentenced to death for undertaking a gun-running expedition intended to support an uprising in Parma by the revolutionary leader Mazzini. Incarcerated in Mantua jail, Orsini quietly channelled his resourcefulness into organising his own escape and early in the morning of 30 March 1856 he knotted together his sheets and clothes, removed the previously sawn bars from his cell window, and lowered himself to the moat. He fled to Switzerland and thence to England.

Arriving in Dover on 26 May 1856, Orsini went straight to London to see Mazzini who had already taken refuge there. Orsini now found that Mazzini was less easily roused to action – he was unable to interest him in his projects but Mazzini did make a practical suggestion. Why did he not write a book about his exploits and his escape from the prison at Mantua? Orsini did so, and much to his surprise, it quickly sold 35,000 copies. With the fame of authorship came the opportunity to give public lectures and throughout that winter Orsini toured England giving talks on his adventures. These were perhaps not as illuminating as they could have been since his English was not of a particularly high standard. However, he was a handsome and striking figure and had an exciting tale to tell.

It is not quite clear at what point Orsini decided to attempt the assassination of Napoleon III, and later, at his trial, his explanation for this plan seemed to lack rationale. Whatever the reasoning, at some time before 1857 he became fixed with the idea that if Napoleon could be disposed of then the next French government would be a people's government rather than a dictatorship and the first thing that they would wish to do would be to withdraw the French garrison from Rome. Orsini wanted a unified Italy. No Italian politician could imagine such a possibility whilst a foreign army sat astride the middle of their peninsula, occupying their most important city.

Orsini began to recruit sympathisers from among the exiles in London, specifically those who were not in Mazzini's circle. Dr Simon Bernard, a French language teacher and elocutionist, had already acted as Orsini's agent for his lecture tours. Dr. Bernard had the added quality of being a proficient amateur chemist. Giuseppe Andrea Pieri, an Italian language teacher living in Birmingham, proved to have had an active past in the French Foreign Legion and the Paris barricades of 1848, the latter earning him expulsion from France. Antonio

Gomez, a young Neapolitan, was short of money and easily persuaded. And Thomas Allsop, an English barrister whom Orsini had first met in Nice. Allsop would facilitate the manufacture of the grenade casings since a foreigner placing such an order with a firm would immediately arouse suspicion. The ruse seems to have succeeded, for the engineer employed, a Mr Taylor of Birmingham, was later to assure the authorities that he had assumed Mr Allsop to be a senior official of the War Office. Finally, Giuseppe di Giorgi, an Italian restaurant worker about to take up post at the Café Suisse in Brussels. He would transport the empty grenades to the Continent where they would be collected, filled with the concoction prepared by Dr Bernard and primed ready for use by Orsini. Everything was set. All Orsini needed was a passport.

The passport of the day was not the neat modern booklet complete with photograph and description with which we are now familiar. It was most likely to be a single sheet of paper, headed by a coat of arms and printed with an ornamental script requesting in florid language that the owner be allowed to pass unhindered in the name of the monarch or state. It would be issued to any applicant who was able to provide an acceptable reference and the requisite fee. The 'Passport System', as it was referred to in the nineteenth century, had as many detractors as promotors.

In Britain, the system was generally reviled by the public. They resented the bureaucracy involved in acquiring a passport, even though it was issued usually within twenty-four hours, and they resented the affront to their dignity in holding a document whose very existence implied that the bona-fides of an English gentleman could ever be put in doubt. Britain did not require of foreigners that they provide themselves with passports in order to disembark on their shores. Unfortunately for the British, two countries through which they had to pass, Belgium and

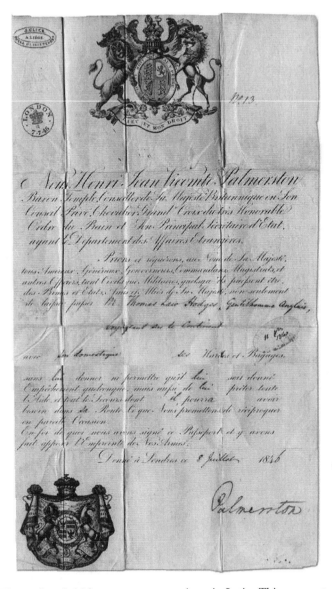

The earliest British passports were written in Latin. This passport, issued in 1846 was written in French and signed personally by the Foreign Secretary, in this case, Palmerston. The only description provided of the holder is *'Gentilhomme Anglais'* – English Gentleman.

France, did require passports, and so the British traveller felt himself even more disadvantaged. An illustration, perhaps, of the authorities' lack of enthusiasm for passports is that no description of an Englishman's physiognomy was required on a British passport until 1915. At the turn of the eighteenth century the lowliest Continental agricultural worker requesting permission to walk 30 miles down the road had to possess a passport describing him down to the colour of his eyebrows and shape of his chin, whereas, a century later, the traveller intending to circumnavigate the globe, could still do so on a document which would proffer such a description as, 'British Subject' or 'English gentleman travelling on the Continent with his wife and servants.'

In France, the 'Passport System' had been well established before the French Revolution of 1789. Internal passports for travel from town to town were required as well as overseas passports for foreign excursions. The system was exploited by the police for the checking and control of foreigners; it was used by the State to prevent skilled workers and capital from leaving and deterring trouble-makers from arriving. When a traveller arrived in a French port he surrendered his passport which was forwarded to Paris and he was issued with a replacement. Upon arrival in the capital, he was obliged to attend the Préfecture de Police to have his original passport viséd for the next series of towns on his journey. The bureaucracy even extended to the hotels where he stayed – the concierge had to submit the passports of his foreign guests to the local police station to be checked and entered in a register.

Orsini was born in the Principality of Piedmont, a state in the north of Italy bordering on France. It was at that time part of the Kingdom of Sardinia and so he applied to the Sardinian Consulate General at 66, Russell Square, London for a passport, giving his reason for travelling as a wish to visit his wife and daughter whom he had left in Nice.

This pretext would ostensibly serve him to cross the Channel at Dover and travel down through France via Paris. Not surprisingly, Orsini and his exploits were well known to the Sardinian authorities. They could not afford to upset such a powerful neighbour as France by granting facilities which would permit a known revolutionary to travel through that country, so, taking the side of caution, they declined to issue him with a passport. They moderated this refusal with the suggestion that if he indeed wanted to visit Nice, which was not a French city but of the Kingdom of Sardinia, then they would issue instructions to the city authorities to admit him and he could go direct by sea from England. How much they had guessed and how much they had suspected of Orsini's intentions we can only surmise but in proposing such a solution they had ostensibly taken his application at face value which had the effect of calling his bluff.

A modern-day traveller would be scandalised to be refused a passport by his own country, especially if the passport were intended to permit him to return home to visit his family. No doubt Orsini was incommoded but this was not the only route to a passport. Strange as it may seem, it was quite legal for any person to go to the French or Belgian consulate and obtain one of their passports for travel. The applicant did not need to be a national of the respective country. The poet Robert Browning for example, when he 'eloped' with his wife Elizabeth Barrett Browning in 1846, probably did so on a French passport. Indeed, with the price of a British passport at that time costing £2 7s 6d (£2.37$^{1}/_2$) and requiring the applicant to either know the Foreign Secretary personally, know someone who did, or have a recommendation from a banking house of repute, it was not surprising that many British subjects availed themselves of foreign passports, especially as these were often issued free of charge.

Whilst the British public considered Orsini's exploits to

be famous, unfortunately for Orsini, the French and Belgian governments regarded them as notorious. There would have been no point in his applying to either of these two countries for a passport. The solution seemed obvious – a false passport.

On 26 November 1857, John Gerard, the Belgian Vice Consul was sitting in his office at 11, Bury Court, St Mary Axe, London when a man brought him a British passport for him to stamp with a Belgian visa. He did not notice the man except that he was a foreigner and that he spoke with a strong Italian accent. This was not in any way suspicious as a gentleman could easily have sent his manservant to the Consulate with the passport. He did notice, however, that the passport had not been signed by the owner and so he asked the man where he was. The man said that he was at the Jamaica Coffee House so the Vice-Consul said that he should attend in person as he could not visé an unsigned passport. 'About ten minutes later', said the Vice-Consul, 'he came. He complained of the trouble he had to come to the office about this passport, stating that he had travelled with it before and never had occasion to be troubled about it.' The Vice-Consul made him sign the passport there and then and he affixed the Belgian visa. He believed him to be an Englishman. 'I made it my business to look at him to be sure he was an Englishman as the passport had travelled six years without being signed.' The name the man signed was, 'T. Allsop'.[1]

Two days later it was the turn of the unsuspecting French Consulate. The same passport was presented to Adolphe Wee who, in affixing the French visa, did not even check whether the passport had been signed or not. On the following day, Felice Orsini bade goodbye to his maid, Eliza Chesney and left his lodgings at 2, Grafton Street. That was the last she saw of him. He next appeared in Brussels at the Hotel de L'Europe, collecting the grenade casings from di Georgi. By 12 December he was in Paris, lodging at a hotel

The Passport Office Register for 15 August 1851 showing the issue of passport no.8197 to 'Thos. Allsop', who was travelling on the Continent. The application was recommended by the bank of Prescott's and the passport cost 7s 6d. This was the passport used by Orsini to enter France and attempt the assassination of Napoleon III in 1858.

in the rue du Mont Thabor under the identity of Thomas Allsop, an Englishman. He had with him his manservant who was travelling on a passport issued by the French Consul on 24 April 1857 to an Englishman called Sweeney. The servant was actually the impecunious Neapolitan, Antonio Gomez. It was he who, unwittingly, was to lead the French police to Orsini.

On the night of the assassination attempt, a remarkable coincidence occurred. Shortly before the Imperial carriage was due, Giuseppe Pieri, the former Foreign Legionnaire who had been previously expelled from France, was getting into position for the attack when he was recognised by a police inspector, M. Hebert. The latter immediately arrested him and took him to the police station where he was searched and his bomb was discovered. Orsini was unaware of this as he counted the explosions. The police inspector, quickly guessing the significance of the bomb, ran back to the Opera to raise the alarm. He was just in time to be injured by the third bomb.

Those who took part in the attack all made their escape during the ensuing chaos. At the pharmacies in the district, as the wounded dribbled in, the rumours ran wild. Orsini calmly queued with the other injured persons and obtained treatment for a head wound then carefully made his way back to the rue du Mont Thabor. Young Gomez was not so sanguine. He was devastated by what he had done. He went into a café and sat at the back with his head in his hands, moaning. When somebody noticed that a pistol had dropped from his pocket, a policeman was sent for and in great agitation Gomez gave his identity as Sweeney, the manservant of an English gentilhomme called Thomas Allsop of the rue du Mont Thabor.

At 2.30 a.m. on 15 January, Inspecteur Michel le Grange hammered on Orsini's door. When Orsini opened it, Le Grange looked over his shoulder and noticed the blood-soaked pillow on the bed. 'Who are you?' the inspector demanded in French. Orsini replied that he was an Englishman. The policeman immediately switched into English. 'Show me your passport.' Orsini handed him the British passport in the name of Thomas Allsop. 'Where do you come from?'

Orsini knew that the real Thomas Allsop lived in Clapham Common. 'Kent', he said.

'How far is that from London?'

'About thirty kilometres.'

'Ha,' said Le Grange, 'if you are an Englishman then I am a Turk. An Englishman would have said, "twenty miles".'

Le Grange arrested Orsini and by the end of that Friday, all the conspirators had been detained. The French public were relieved to learn that none of their countrymen had been involved in the attempt but were angry to discover that the Italian exiles had plotted their conspiracy safely in England. When it later was revealed that the bombs had been manufactured in Birmingham, a great public indignation arose, as ardent as it was irrational. The feeling was that England should eject its dangerous exiles; this was avoiding the obvious question, where to? If the Piedmontese authority would not issue a passport for one of its own nationals to return home, which country would have accepted him? Where could he have been ejected to?

In the French press, *Le Moniteur*, which was almost the official organ of the State, published addresses from the Army implying that England was instrumental in the attack and one colonel of a regiment of the line went as far as to address the Emperor demanding to be 'led against that lair, that den, the nest of homicide,'[2] meaning England.

The British Prime Minister, Lord Palmerston had, in a previous administration, held the office of Foreign Secretary and was very much alive to the harm that could be done to Franco-British relations by injudicious comments. He tried to ease the British public to an understanding of the reason for the French ill will. He pointed out that had foreign exiles plotted in France, armed themselves with French bombs and French passports and then entered England and made an attempt upon the life of our Queen Victoria, then we would almost certainly feel exactly as the French do now. One of Palmerston's former duties as Foreign Secretary had been to sign the passports issued in his name and, rather embarrassingly, the Thomas Allsop passport that Orsini had used to enter France bore his signature.

Ineluctably the parameters of the debate were widened and the Passport System itself was put under scrutiny. The practice whereby the French and Belgian governments issued passports to British Subjects was seized upon as being tantamount to an encouragement to conspiracy and fraud. Foreign Consuls did not enquire as to the character of applicants, it was pointed out. A few months before the Orsini affair, some disreputable English characters had taken out French passports and travelled to Paris to rob various jewellers. They had been arrested at Southampton upon their return, still in possession of the jewels. On other occasions, unemployed workmen who would not normally have been able to afford a Foreign Office passport had taken the cheaper French passports and crossed the Channel in the belief that work was abundant there. They had been misinformed and it had fallen to the British Government to pay for their repatriation.[3] These priggish accusations implied that the propriety of an Englishman's character was established by the mere existence of his

Passengers' passports being examined as they disembark from the Channel packet at Dieppe during the Franco-Prussian War, 1871.

Foreign Office passport. How unfortunate it was then, that Orsini had held one such passport.

The French Governement announced on 5 February 1858, that it was ceasing immediately the arrangement whereby it issued passports to British subjects. The Earl of Clarendon, the British Secretary of State for Foreign Affairs, indicated that he welcomed this move and wished other countries would follow suit. Two days earlier he had enlarged the group of people who could recommend an applicant for a Foreign Office Passport to include mayors, chief magistrates of corporate towns in the United Kingdom, magistrates and justices of the peace. This was necessary to absorb the greater demand expected from the increase in the number of applicants. The charge for a passport was now six shillings (30p.) regardless of the number of people mentioned on the document.

The Foreign Secretary's contentment was short lived. Two weeks later the French Government also withdrew the 'no-passport' concession for British subjects. This was an arrangement that particularly favoured the towns of Dover and Folkestone in England and their counterpart ports in France – Calais and Boulogne. Under the system, tourists only intending to visit the town and not enter France proper, were not required to obtain a passport. There was a considerable traffic under this concession; approximately 100,000 passengers annually took excursion train trips to Calais or Boulogne at that time and both these ports had (and still have) a large settlement of British nationals. The withdrawal of the concession meant that every person disembarking was now required to hold a Foreign Office passport whether they intended visiting France or merely the quayside cafés in Calais. The results were chaotic. British subjects were refused entry to France and put back on the ship. In Le Havre, a port which received 5,000 visitors per year, the British Consul, Mr Featherstonhaugh, had to intercede when the French authorities would not allow a ship loaded with passportless passengers to discharge.[4] The packet boat companies suddenly found themselves dealing with passenger loads counted in tens instead of in hundreds. The traders of Calais and Boulogne tightened their belts and the British residents in those ports found that they could no longer travel outside the town in which they had lived for years unless they held a passport.

The campaign in the French and British press continued apace. The situation was of a legal nicety which evinced learned debate in the newspapers. A foreigner had taken exile in England and had plotted to commit a crime upon another foreigner to be perpetrated abroad. Wherein lay the criminal responsibility of Britain? Palmerston's efforts at conciliation were doomed to failure from the start by the differing administrative backgrounds of the two countries. The French people were accustomed to having to prove their identity upon demand and could not understand how such dangerous exiles and conspirators could be allowed to walk the streets freely unless there were some tacit indulgence on the part of the British Government.

In a letter to the editor entitled, 'How We Come To Have Refugees in England', one reader of *The Times* recounted an incident he had experienced in France and made a tentative but quite accurate suggestion.

'Sir,
    The summer before last, while residing with my family at Boulogne, I witnessed on two or three occasions the shipment of batches of Italian refugees on board the Folkestone boat for delivery in England.
    I was particularly struck by one lot who were brought down to the harbour escorted by a large body of police. Judging from the extreme attention shown them by their guardians and the number of those who were linked, in no affectionate bonds to the wrist of their conductors, I concluded that the party would form a very pretty additionto English society. Two or three of them appeared men of education, and most of

them were of the exact type which formed, in Cassius' eyes, the perfected conspirator. Several of them had hunches of black bread in their hands. All of them were buttoned up in rags and half-famished in appearance. What I learnt of them was, that they had been passed on from police station to police station, and were not wanted in France.

I well remember the insulting gestures and coarse oaths which were flung at the gendarmerie as the boat left the quay and felt satisfied from the violence of one or two of them that had the means been in their hands they would have left with those gentry some more definite token of their opinion of France and its authorities.

Some six weeks afterwards I twice met two of these men still buttoned up in their rags, but as erect and defiant as ever, parading in Piccadilly.

Do you not think it possible that this lot might have furnished a band for the rue Lepelletier business?'[5]

However near to the truth the observation might have been, the letter was indicative of the popular antagonism between France and Britain at the time. Palmerston was well aware of the need to smooth international relations. Believing the country to be behind him, he proposed in the House of Commons a Conspiracy to Murder bill.

...A conspiracy has been formed, partly in this country for the purpose of committing a most atrocious crime. That conspiracy has led to most disastrous consequences... the law in this country – in England – treats a conspiracy to murder simply as a misdemeanour subject to a fine and a short period of imprisonment... the conspiracy to murder is punishable on the same level and in the same manner as a conspiracy for any other purpose such as hissing at the theatre.'[6]

Palmerston identified the public's anger at what it saw as meddling by the French government in the internal affairs of Britain. '...a disposition prevails on the Continent in general that the Government and Parliament of this country should take some steps which should place it in the power of the Government, on mere suspicion, to remove aliens from the UK.'[7] Despite explaining that this was not the intention of his government and that he would not be swayed by foreign pressure, Palmerston failed to settle the turmoil. Opposition was virulent and he had miscalculated his support.

His opponents pointed out that assassination was not an English crime, it was a foreign crime. The assassins had come from England but before that, they had come to England from foreign countries run by governments whose behaviour had made their own subjects into assassins. Napoleon III had enjoyed the hospitality of England whilst plotting to take the power in France and no English king had fallen by the hand of the assassin although kings of France had. The submission of the latter observation was qualified with the rider that, of course we had occasionally executed a monarch, but that was different.

The debate ranged over two nights. The popular feeling which Palmerston had so misread was summed up in the arguments: 'If England wishes to hold her place among the nations, if she wishes still to maintain her own independent position, no solicitation of an ally, no threatenings on the part of anybody ought to lead us to alter our laws.'[8] and: 'The will of a foreign monarch ought not to be the standard of English Law.'[9]

The Conspiracy to Murder bill was defeated at the second reading by 234 votes to 215 on 19 February 1858 and Palmerston's government was forced to resign which it did on the 22nd. As a result of the Thomas Allsop passport used in the assassination attempt, the protocol for issuing passports was changed for all time; it was never to return to the situation where one state could issue a passport which claimed the authority to identify the holder as a national of another state. No longer could an Englishman travel abroad on a legally issued Belgian or French passport.

And what of Count Felice Orsini who had caused all this trouble? Almost unnoticed in the British press, he had been committed for trial at the Assize Court of the Seine on 12 February, found guilty and executed a month later. But the final word on this affair of conspiracy and assassination, false passports and counter accusations must really go to the intended victim himself. Napoleon III had already published an appraisal of the liberty of the individual in England in one of his works. It stands as a pragmatic and perceptive analysis of the effectiveness of the Passport System:

'In England the first of all liberties, that of going where you please, is never disturbed for there no-one is asked for passports. Passports – the oppressive invention of the Committee of Public Safety which are an embarrassment and an obstacle to the peaceable citizen but which are utterly powerless against those who wish to deceive the vigilance of authority.'[10]

2

The First Passport

Although some would regard the Europe of Orsini's day as the romantic heyday of the passport, it would be wrong to believe that the passport was first introduced in the mid-nineteenth century or that the Passport System which he had upset had been the product of one contemporary brain, administration or power. Passports had existed long before then. What did occur in the nineteenth century was a great expansion in popular travel. This forced governments to review and formalise the passport procedures which had evolved gradually over centuries of wars and diplomacies, treaties and trades.

Whereas formerly it had been quite possible, if a little divisive, for passports to be issued personally by the Foreign Secretary only to persons with whom he was acquainted, once the masses started to move, this procedure was shown to be utterly inadequate. During the nineteenth century the widespread replacement of the handwritten document with the pre-printed passport took place.

But even this was merely another stage in the continuing evolution of the passport. Throughout history, the passport document has been changed and adapted to meet the varying demands made upon it. Many of these early documents were not called passports – the laissez-passer, the safe conduct – and some documents which called themselves passports we would not today recognise in that form. We tend to think of a passport simply as something a person needs in order to travel but this ignores the fact that passports and their ancestors are also concerned with such concepts as identity, nationality and allegiance. And they were not only issued to facilitate the passage of persons; they have been issued to goods to allow them to be moved from a country. Sir Horace Mann, the British Minister in Florence, Italy, writing to the English novelist Horace Walpole on 5 June 1743 mentions a third party, who, '...not being willing to lose his furniture he ordered his agent to ask me to get him a passport for its safe passage to some Spanish port.'[1] Long before this, passports had been issued to ships; indeed so well established in the realms of commerce was the ship's passport that pre-printed forms in various languages were already available in the sixteenth century.

A 'Passport for Foreign Ships' issued by the French Customs in the name of the King of the French on 24 June 1845 to the American three-masted ship, 'Alabama' of 697 tons, permitting her to depart the port of Le Havre with a mixed cargo, bound for New York.

The word 'passport' is first found in English acts of law in 1548 and in this context referred to a document which concerned the regulation of soldiers and wars. 'No captain shall give to any of his soldiers appointed to serve under him in any town or fortress kept with garrisons of soldiers any licence or passport to depart from his service...'[2] The passport mentioned in this case was what we would nowadays describe as an army leave pass.

The word 'passport' itself has obscure origins. At first examination its sense would seem self-evident. It was a document used to allow the bearer to pass through a port, either to enter or leave a territory. French being the language of international diplomacy, it probably comes from the French *passer* meaning 'to pass' and *port* meaning 'port'. But a passport was also used to travel within a country, often from one town to another. Towns had walls with gates in them which were locked at night and through which you could not pass as a stranger without your passport; and the French word for the gate is *porte*. In the example of 1548 above, the milieu is that of fortresses, towns and garrisons, there is no suggestion of ships, seas and ports and yet the word 'passport' is used.

Understanding now that the definition of a passport is not restricted uniquely to documents bearing that name, the search for the first passport is no longer a simple case of finding the oldest document in the world which is called a passport, and the question of when the first passport was issued becomes less easy to answer. Writing was first invented about 3000 BC, probably in Mesopotamia, and it is possible to hypothesise that no passport could have been issued prior to that. The earliest forms of writing were the ideograph and cuneiform scripts which have been discovered inscribed on stone tablets in various sites in the Middle East. But stone tablets were not the only form of writing available, merely the most durable and they were certainly unsuited for a document which needed to be carried often and easily. An official document would probably have been engraved by a scribe using a pointed stylus on a wooden or ivory tablet which had been prepared with a coating of wax. The Victorian Egyptologist, Sir J. Gardner Wilkinson affirms that it is recorded that around 1500BC the common people in Egypt were required to register themselves with the magistrates: 'It appears that they not only enrolled their names and gave in the various particulars required of them, but were obliged to have a passport from the magistrate... for a document of that kind was required for every ship quitting a port.'[3] He further suggests that the drawings found in a tomb at Thebes represent people being registered before the magistrate and then coming before the scribes to have their passports issued.

Egyptian drawings from a tomb at Thebes, 1600 BC.
People appear to be coming to be registered and (below)
are being issued with a passport-type document.

There is also evidence of the existence of passports in the Bible, Old Testament. Nehemiah required documents for his journey: '...Moreover I said unto the King, if it pleases the King let letters be given me to the governors beyond the river that they may convey me over till I come into Judah... Then I came to the governors beyond the river and gave them the King's letters...'[4]

Nehemiah was travelling from Shushan in Susiana to Jerusalem in Palestine in about 450 BC. The present day equivalent of this journey would be from Iraq to Israel. A passport that could facilitate such a journey nowadays would be a rare document indeed. The form of the letters given to Nehemiah by King Artaxerxes is not specified but we can identify in their intended use, the common ancestry of all passports. However, deciding who issued the first passport and to whom will probably have to remain forever mere speculation.

Whatever the first passport was issued for, one thing is certain: it must have been linked with travel. Without travel the primary purpose of a passport is lost but a passport device can only exist if the social intercourse within the relevant societies is sufficiently developed to permit it to function. Travellers discovered that a very effective way of protecting themselves when venturing abroad was to arm themselves with a letter issued by a powerful person in their own country. By its very existence such a document constituted a discreet threat of heavy reprisals should anything untoward happen to the bearer. The weight of its argument could be increased considerably if the letter were also addressed to an equally powerful person in the country of destination.

The earliest passports would only have existed where there was a developed society with recognised channels of intercourse. The Romans created the largest empire the world had seen at that time and maintained it not only with an efficient Army but also a sophisticated civil service.

The Army maintained the Roman Peace within the Empire and this stability allowed travel to develop within an ordered framework.

To ensure the rapid communications with Rome which were vital for governing such an extensive empire, the Emperor Augustus Caesar set up the Imperial Post. Between the various important cities, small stations were established and provided with the necessaries of travel: horses, asses, vehicles and slaves, which were only available for the use of the Emperor, his servants and messengers. All other officials required special authorisation by the reigning emperor and this authority was embodied in a document issued to them called a *tractorium*. It was in the form of a tablet, folding into two parts, which carried the name of the reigning emperor, the name of the holder and the length of time for which it was valid. A stock of signed and dated blanks were sent to each provincial governor for issue as needed. The blanks were not allowed to be issued after their expired date and when the emperor died, then the permission died with him and the *tractorium* lost its authority.

Like any system of prerogative, those operating it were sometimes tempted to bend the rules to their own ends. Records show that the Younger Pliny informed the Emperor Trajan that he had issued a *tractorium* to his own wife to facilitate a visit to a relative in need; fortune shone on Pliny, for the emperor wrote back with his approval.[5]

In time, the Roman Empire crumbled and with it, the system which had ensured the need for the *tractoria*. The next few centuries in British history were an unsettled time characterised by foreign invasion and subjugation of the indigenous population. A *tractorium*-type document which assured its holder of assistance, food and horses and by extension, conferred upon him a certain prestige, had no place in this period of upheaval but this was not to say that passport tokens of some sort were not used.

With wars come peace negotiations and the delegates to such parleys quite sensibly concern themselves first of all with procedures to guarantee their own safety. Without the promise that they would be allowed to leave the enemy camp and return to their own lines, their attendance at any sort of discussion would be dangerous and pointless. The system which evolved was for the visiting negotiators to be given the promise of an unmolested passage and to confirm the authenticity of the promise, they were given hostages from the other side who were released once the negotiators were back safely in their own lines. This promise was encapsulated in a document called a 'safe conduct' and was certainly in use in 1051 when King Edward the Confessor's brother-in-law, Eustace of Boulogne visited England.

On his return journey, Eustace had a contretemps with the residents of Dover which left about twenty dead on each side. The King ordered the Saxon Earl Godwin to ravage Dover as punishment but Godwin refused. By this act he played into the hands of the King's Norman supporters and they encouraged the King to consider Godwin's behaviour as a case of rebellion.

Edward called a meeting of the Witenagemot – the council of wise men who took the decisions relating to the running of the country. Godwin was required to attend. He arrived with his sons Harold and Sweyn. When he asked for hostages to provide surety for his life, the King insisted that his thanes surrender their allegiance to the person of the King. This now left Godwin unsupported. He was told to present himself with twelve men but he refused because the surety of hostages that he had demanded was not forthcoming and so he was given five days to leave the kingdom.

The account of these events in the *Anglo Saxon Chronicle* can be expected to show bias against the Norman line but it is interesting nonetheless for the reference to the working of the safe conduct system:

'Then Swegen earl was proclaimed an outlaw and Godwine earl, and Harold earl were summoned to the meeting as quickly as they might come to it. And when they came thither [to London] then they were summoned to the meeting. Then he [Godwine] asked for safe conduct and hostages that he might come securely into the meeting and out of the meeting. Then the king asked for all the thanes whom the earls had had, and they gave them all into his hand. Then the king sent again to them and bade them come to the king's council with twelve men. Then again the earl asked for safe conduct and hostages and was given a safe conduct for five nights to leave the land. Then Godwine earl and Swegen earl went to Boshan and launched their ships and betook themselves beyond the sea and sought the protection of Baldwin and dwelt there all winter....'[6]

Bosham near Chichester in West Sussex was at that time an important port. It has a Norman church and tradition claims that one of the daughters of Canute is buried there.

Complementary to the idea of the safe conduct to give a person secure passage from a kingdom, is the King's Licence to permit a person to enter or leave the kingdom. When William of Normandy invaded England in 1066 to be crowned William I, one of the first things that he did was to build castles to prevent anybody else from doing what he had just done. He also began to dilute the Saxon influence in the Church and to this end he invited Pope Alexander II to send legates to England to set up Synods. Many of the Saxon bishops, including Stigand the Archbishop of Canterbury, were deposed and the church was remodelled on stricter lines of discipline and learning.

William I was able to invite legates to his kingdom because he had put in place an early system of immigration control. Nobody could land without the King's Licence and the ports were now overseen by his newly constructed castles which could be garrisoned expressly to enforce this requirement.

Ironically, some of the first beneficiaries of this system were to be amongst its first victims, for William soon argued with Rome and a few years later, in 1078, he issued an instruction to the keepers of his castles to prevent any legates from Pope Gregory VII from landing without the King's Licence.[7]

The King's Licence requirement was continued by William's successors and in the reign of Henry I in 1115, one more papal legate fell foul of it. Anselm, a nephew of the eponymous archbishop, tried to disembark in Dover without the King's Licence. He was prevented from landing and forced to return to Wissant in France. This must be one of the earliest recorded cases of a traveller being refused entry under an immigration system.

The King's Licence, like the Saxon safe conduct mentioned earlier, would have been a document written in Latin. Before the arrival of the Normans, legal documents such as grants of land or favours, were written in Latin although the laws were published in Saxon English and the judicial cases conducted in that language. After the Norman invasion of England the language of the courts was changed to French but the laws were still published in English. Although William could trace his ancestry back a century and a half in France, he did all his administrative work either in Latin or English.

So a twelfth-century traveller possessed a document which proclaimed that he had the personal permission of the monarch to travel. This suggests that the frequency of travel had changed such that it was now practical to have documents issued by one person upon demand instead of prepared beforehand as the Romans had done eight centuries earlier.

The monarch would be particularly interested in who wished to leave his kingdom. If his subjects had developed particular skills, the acquisition or knowledge of which might benefit his enemies, such as the making of longbows

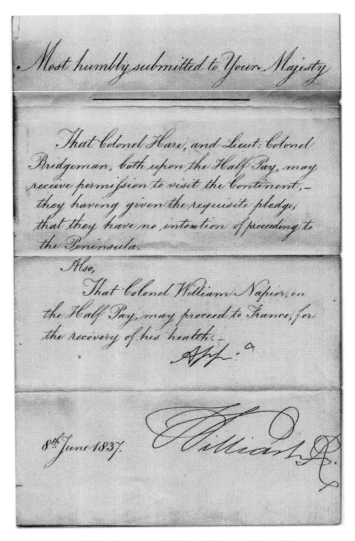

Most humbly submitted to Your Majesty

That Colonel Hare, and Lieut: Colonel Bridgeman, both upon the Half Pay, may receive permission to visit the Continent,— they having given the requisite pledge, that they have no intention of proceeding to the Peninsula.

Also,

That Colonel William Napier, on the Half Pay, may proceed to France, for the recovery of his health:—

8th June 1837.

The shaky signature 'William R' was endorsed on this document by King William IV, twelve days before his death on 20 June 1837.

It grants the King's Licence to three army officers to visit the Continent, subject to certain conditions.

for example, then it would not be wise for such people to depart his realm. Also, by leaving the kingdom each subject was depriving the king of his services, be they feudal or military. Paradoxically, in the matter of enemies within the kingdom, it was considered safer to keep them in the country than to let them travel abroad since, once overseas, they might raise an army of supporters and return to press their point of view more forcibly.

Earl Godwin, after having used his five days' safe conduct to go to Ireland in 1051, did indeed return the following year with several ships and a small body of men. He was still popular with the common people and Edward the Confessor, finding himself in the weaker position, was obliged to pardon him his misdemeanours.

But intending treachery and selling defence secrets are not commonplace stimuli to the desire for travel; the one certain stimulus which moved our ancestors was the wish or the need to trade. Even during the bitterest wars and bloodiest conflicts, traders were still active, indeed, in some circumstances, trading with the enemy was not entirely proscribed. The importance of international trade was recognised in the Magna Carta. This document was signed reluctantly by King John of England in 1215 at the insistence of a committee of citizens and influential barons. In establishing the rights of an Englishman it also serves as a fine contemporary indicator to the state of the realm. Clause 48 decrees: 'all merchants shall have safe and secure conduct to go out of, and come into England and to stay there and to pass, as well by land as by water.'8

This concession was further extended to the ordinary population by clause 50: 'It shall be lawful for the time to come for anyone to go out of our kingdom and return safely and securely by land or by water, saving his allegiance to us unless in time of war for some short space for the common benefit of the kingdom, except prisoners and outlaws and people in wars with us and merchants who shall be in such condition as is above mentioned.'⁹ This was a volte-face to section III of the Constitutions of Clarendon of 1164 which decreed that: 'No person of any rank whatever [is] to be permitted to leave the realm without the royal licence.'¹⁰

The King's Licence system and the provisions of the Magna Carta were all very fine in theory but the practice was somewhat different. When Henry II signed the Constitutions of Clarendon in 1164 he was trying to sort out his trouble with Archbishop Thomas à Becket. He failed and the Constitutions soon fell into disuse. The Magna Carta, in its turn, was disregarded by King John who refused to apply its conditions and although the Charter was written, rewritten and reaffirmed several times in the following years, its effects were quite limited. Despite its claim to stand for all time, succeeding monarchs did not necessarily consider themselves bound by it.

The practical application of the King's Licence system relied upon the banned person embarking or arriving in a port overseen by one of the monarch's castles but this surveillance could be sidestepped by landing at a minor creek or by owning your own port such as Pevensey, owned by John O'Gaunt. In 1170, at the height of Henry II's dispute with the Church, for example, Henry ordered the Constable of Dover to seize Becket if he landed. Becket simply came ashore a few miles further up the coast at the port of Sandwich which belonged to Canterbury Cathedral of which he was the archbishop.

Arguing as they did against the prerogative of the King's Licence, the clauses of the Magna Carta stand as an early attempt to abolish a passport system. If it was the first attempt to fail, it would not be the last.

3

ALIENS WITHIN, MACHIAVELLI WITHOUT

In 1389 London Bridge consisted of a stone gate and wooden drawbridge leading to a series of stone arches thrown across the river. On top of these, perched wooden built houses and shops on a decking which overlapped either side to be supported by massive timbers from beneath. The carriageway of the bridge was nowhere more than 20 feet wide, in several parts it was narrower, and in places the upper storeys of the buildings had been built across to the opposite side to form a sort of tunnel. Not the ideal location for a joust and yet, on St George's day, 23 April 1389, two massive chargers, each carrying a knight in armour with lance at the ready, faced each other along the length of London Bridge.

The occupants of the houses on the bridge hung from their windows, enjoying a bird's eye view whilst outside the Bear at the Bridge Foot Tavern the revellers jostled and shoved for any kind of glimpse of the action. In the outrageous splendour of the era, King Richard II and his court were safely installed on a dais which had been especially built for the purpose of watching the joust.

At the signal of the heralds, the knights raising their lances and the carriageway of the bridge rang with the noise of the hooves as the two horses thundered towards each other. On one sat Lord Welles, the English Ambassador to Scotland and on the other, Sir David de Lindesay, a Scot. How had this extraordinary affair come about?

It had all started with an argument – not a violent disagreement but more of a provocative teasing by Lord John Welles during a banquet in Scotland. An active and forthright man and accustomed to airing his opinions whatever the cost, he had raised the discussion of which race was the more courageous – the Scots or the English. Being an Englishman himself, he had made it clear that as the English were undoubtedly imbued with more courage than the Scots, anybody wishing to disagree with him would have to prove it on the jousting field. This remark he had aimed at Sir David de Lindesay who had probably been holding his own in the argument particularly well.

We know why the challenge took place on St George's Day – it was chosen by de Lindesay because St George was the patron saint of soldiers – but can we even begin to guess why Lord Welles chose London Bridge as the location? Whatever the reason, the King gave his permission and the preparations were made. In order for de Lindesay to be allowed into England with his attendants, horses, weapons and armour, Welles guaranteed that they would not become a charge on public funds and that he would provide for them to return to Scotland.

The safe conduct was issued on 22 January 1389 to be valid for two months from 1 April:

> The King to all and singular, our Sheriffs, Mayors, Bailifs, Ministers and faithful subjects, within and without our liberties, to whom these present letters shall come, Greeting. Know ye that because our beloved and faithful John Welles, for the perfecting of a certain Passage of Arms within our Kingdom of England, against David de Lyndeseye of Scotland, Knight, as he appears to have calumniated by the said David he is a petitioner to us for the security of the said David, with his followers and servants coming into our Kingdom aforesaid, for the cause aforesaid, and graciously to provide for their remaining here, and returning again to their own country.[1]

The spectators on the bridge cared nought for this as the two enormous horses charged towards each other; this was a free spectacle and they vociferously supported whichever party they fancied. At the first pass, contact was made and the crowd ducked as both lances shattered. The knights reined in their chargers at the opposite ends of the bridge and furnished themselves with new lances. At this point one of the crowd shouted out that the Scotsman must have been locked in the saddle for he had sat so firmly in place at the first strike. Hearing this, de Lindesay jumped down from his horse and then up into the saddle again to disprove the flippant charge. This feat, achieved whilst encased in the full plate armour of the time, impressed the crowd immensely.

The knights spurred up their horses and then hurtled towards each other. The crowd cheered and again the clash broke the knights' lances. A second time they wheeled their chargers around and took new lances. At the third pass, there was an enormous crash and Lord Welles was unseated and was seen to fall heavily to the ground. The crowd groaned, fearing that he had been killed. De Lindesay quickly dismounted and, hurrying to where he lay, tended him until the doctor arrived.

Every day thereafter the Scot visited Welles' sick bed and the King asked him to remain in London. His permit was renewed at Westminster on 13 May and again on the 25 May. Finally a warrant was issued for his departure on the *Seinte Maire* of Dundee, captained by William Snelle. De Lindesay's chivalrous behaviour and subsequent popularity served him well for in 1406, he was named ambassador to England as the Earl of Crawford.

This colourful occasion could have been drawn directly from a child's storybook but, true though it was, it was not typical of the contemporary diplomacy. The chivalry and politeness displayed was a common trend in the interstate negotiations of the time but these qualities often contrasted starkly with the brutality of the warfare practised.

The safe conduct pass or sauf conduit was by now recognised as a parallel concept to the passport. It served the same purpose as a passport – it was to enable persons to travel. But whereas a passport was issued by a country to its subjects, a safe conduct was generally issued by a country to its enemy representative, be he envoy or ambassdor, to grant him safe passage in and out of the kingdom for the purpose of his negotiations. And the rules for the issue and handling of such documents were beginning to appear in an official form. The Baltic state of Lithuania, for example, in drawing up its Statute in 1529, explained the penalties for mishandling safe conducts: 'If someone delivers to someone our safe conduct papers issued at his request, be this to prince or lord or to noble or zemianin to zemianin, whoever of these having read the papers retains them and does not wish to return them then, must pay his gracious king a fine of twelve rubles of grosh.... and the safe conduct papers must be handed over...'[2]

The Lithuanian equivalent of the King's Licence is contained in section III paragraph 8 of the same statute: 'The Sovereign allows everyone to freely leave the Royal Land for training in knighthood to any lands other than enemy lands.'[3]

Documents such as passports and safe conducts could only function in an atmosphere of mutual international recognition and within the burgeoning structure of diplomacy. The technique of sending ambassadors to represent one country's interests to another was a well established system in Ancient Greece and was variously adopted or rejected by succeeding civilisations. The Italians introduced the innovation that led the world into the school of diplomacy that we practise today. Until the fifteenth century, ambassadors were sent abroad for a specific purpose; perhaps to negotiate a marriage or a treaty or some trade advantage or other. Once they had achieved

The safe conduct has been employed in time of war to entice the enemy soldier to defect by guaranteeing him a safe passage to the opposing side.

Above is an imitation Iraqi banknote dropped by air during the first Gulf War and left, is a safe conduct used by the allies in World War 2.

their goal, or in default of success, when they no longer had a purpose, they were withdrawn and returned to their native country. If a country needed a contact or source of information in the court of a foreign power then it would probably first approach a member of that court with a proposal of financial reward for information.

The Italian City States such as Venice and Milan had probably the most efficient information-gathering system in the world. Their intimate knowledge of the goings-on in commerce and royal courts throughout Europe gained them an unassailable position in the world of finance and trade and in order to maintain this in 1452 they introduced a novel concept: the permanent ambassador. Henceforth the ambassador would not be an ephemeral representative but would establish himself in a permanent embassy in the other country.

Italy became the dynamo for this developing discipline and did more than any country to promote the principle of ambassadors with the associated immunity for themselves, their families, servants and baggage. An international common-sense began to be recognised and developed into a foundation for international law.

In 1513 Machiavelli published his treatise entitled *The Prince* and introduced a new slant to the role of a ruler. Up until then the contemporary idea was that a king should try to do all that he could to be thought of as a good king. Machiavelli proposed the startlingly pertinent idea that some of the qualities currently considered as being desirable in a good monarch were not necessarily those which made him a successful ruler and really what he ought to concentrate on was how to be an effective ruler and this would make him a good one. Ruthlessness and deceit were permitted in relations with other countries and even with one's own ambassadors if by doing so it served the overall purpose of the country.

The responsibility for issuing passports in foreign lands

naturally fell to that country's representative and the conduct of these ambassadors must have been affected by Machiavelli's writings. Queen Elizabeth I of England would certainly have had access to his works and it would seem that in applying the principles she did not hesitate to use her licence system as a tool of deceit.

In 1559, James Hamilton the third Earl of Arran, escaped from France to England. His escape suited Elizabeth's designs admirably. The French ambassador, Noailles, knowing only that Arran had escaped, called on Queen Elizabeth and reminded her that if Arran arrived in England he was to be arrested and returned to France under the provisions of the Cateau-Cambresis treaty of friendship between France and Spain. Elizabeth assured him that she would. What she concealed from him was that she had already received Arran secretly in her royal apartments in Greenwich and had then sent him with Thomas Randolph to assist Sir Ralph Sadler's secret mission to stir up trouble in Scotland. In order to remain incognito, the two men had travelled on false passports, Arran in the name of 'de Beaufort' and Randolph, 'Barnabee'.[4]

When it suited her Elizabeth I would even refuse passports to another monarch. The year after Arran escaped, Mary Queen of Scots became a widow. She had been living in France since her early childhood whilst her mother, Mary of Guise, had ruled Scotland as regent. Mary Queen of Scots now wished to return to Scotland. She sent her envoy to the court of Queen Elizabeth I to request that she be issued with a safe conduct pass to transit England en route for Scotland. Not only did Elizabeth refuse to allow the envoy himself a passport for Scotland, she also refused to grant Mary her licence. Upon hearing of this refusal, Mary remarked to the English Ambassador in Paris that she did not need Elizabeth's permission to return to her own country and was sure she could do without her passport or licence, and to prove it she sailed direct from France to Scotland.[5]

Sometimes levity crept in to the tension and jealousy of sixteenth-century diplomacy, even if unintended. In the same year, Prince Eric, the son of the King of Sweden who rather considered himself as a suitor to Elizabeth, wrote her what was in effect a love letter after a shipwreck had prevented him from reaching England. He assured her that he would set out again the following spring and at her simple bidding would defeat no end of enemies if only she would forward a safe conduct, with certain clauses to the effect that he would not be compelled to agree to anything, and be allowed to leave England when he liked without having to sign anything. Perhaps he was right to be suspicious of Elizabeth.[6]

It was customary for the monarch to give a gift to a departing ambassador and on occasions ambassadors would show a little spirit when they saw that they were on sure ground or near it. When the Spanish ambassador, the Count de Feria, was replaced by the Bishop of Aquila in 1559 he suggested to Elizabeth that instead of a gift she should give him, 'a passport for passage to Flanders of all the monks, friars, and nuns now here who were required to renounce their profession, swear against the Pope and observe the articles lately enacted against the Christian and Catholic Church.'[7]

The precision that the Elizabethans searched for in drawing up their passports is evident in a letter from Mary de Guise to Queen Elizabeth requesting a passport for Lord Seton. In it she attempts to cover all the categories of place of arrival and all the means of transport available to him and his retinue and baggage. Interesting also is the proposal that the passport should have a period of validity and be available for multiple journeys – both characteristics being remarkable by their absence from British passports three centuries later:

Richt excellent, richt high and mychtie Princes, oure derrest sustir and ally, We commend ws to yow in oure maist hartlie maner, praying yow to grant, at yis our requisitionn, youre salfconduit and sure pasport in dew forme to George Lorde Seytonn and with him twelf servandis in company, saulflie to cum within youre realme of Inglannd to ony toun, port, havin, burne, creak or parte yairof, one hors or one fute, be sey, launde or fresche watter and to remane thairin, pas and repas throw ye samyn, to and fra ye partis of Fraunce, als oft as he sall think expedient, with yir horsses as weill staint as geldingis, bulgettis, cofferis, caskettis, fardellis, gold, silver, connyett and uncunnyett, and lettars, clos and patent, without ony serche, arreist, stop, trowble or impediment to be maid or done to yame or ony of yame, at ony toun, port, passaige or parte of youre realme and dominions, for ye space of ane yeir...[8]

If Elizabeth was Machiavellian in the application of her royal Licence, she was nonetheless assisted in her deceits and manoeuvres by her able and trusted royal Secretary, Francis Walsingham. He performed various diplomatic tasks for his monarch but perhaps his most useful was the setting up of his system of spies and control to counter the plots and designs of Elizabeth's enemies.

Part of Walsingham's intelligence-gathering operation was undertaken at the ports. When a young Wurtemburger Samuel Kiechel arrived in England from Ulm in the 1580s it was to Walsingham's agents that the travellers were obliged to report. He recounted that as soon as they landed at Dover they were summoned before these men who demanded to know where they came from, where they were going and what was their business. They had been forced to show all their letters, whether open or sealed and he claimed that even official couriers were not exempt from this.[9] Any present-day traveller unfortunate enough to experience difficulty with the passport officer will see instant parallels between this sixteenth-century account and the treatment which can be meted out at modern frontier controls.

On occasions Walsingham himself issued the passport. When Leopold Von Wedel arrived in England from Pomerania in 1584 he expressed a desire to visit Scotland for which he needed to obtain a passport. Unfortunately the royal Court was in residence in Oatlands Palace, near Weybridge in Surrey, some miles south of London. Dragging his interpreter along with him, Von Wedel made his way out to the court. There he was interviewed by Walsingham himself who then issued him with a passport for Scotland. Von Wedel rather smugly reports that the courtiers who were standing nearby had observed that he had been fortunate because passports had often been refused because the Queen and the Scots were not seeing eye to eye at that time.[10]

Already it can be seen that the purpose of a passport had begun to subtly change. In the earliest times it was an introduction, a protection and a facilitation. As the rule of monarchs became more established, the passport was recognised as a tool to control a population, be they your subjects wishing to leave or those of another allegiance wishing to come in. But there was another group of persons, a minority whose growing influence was to make some sort of regulation necessary – aliens already in the country.

Distinctive groups of foreigners had settled in England in the wake of every invasion. Celts, Angles, Saxons and Danes had intermingled into one cohesive race by the time of William I's invasion which brought not only the Normans but also the Jews to England. Then came the Flemish clothworkers, encouraged by Henry I to forsake Flanders and settle in England to practise their skills.

In 1190 the Jews were expelled en masse after a murderous public uprising against them, and were to be banished until 1656. In the interim, a succession of monarchs encouraged the settlement of Flemish woollen workers and craftsmen, Italian and German merchants and eventually, after the return of the Jews, Protestant Huguenots fleeing persecution on the Continent.

Throughout the Middle Ages the welcome afforded foreigners in England was, at the least, ambiguous. The Crown encouraged alien merchants and bankers to trade in England. In fact without the Lombardy and Hanseatic financiers, much of the commercial development of England would have been quite impossible; and the expenditure needed to undertake many of the wars would have been unsustainable. The merchants and craftsmen brought tremendous resources to the country, particularly with their skills in the woollen trade and they generated much wealth and yet much legislation seems to have been enacted during this time with the express purpose of disadvantaging foreign workers practising in England and in making the imports of foreign wares unattractive.

Usually aliens had to pay a higher duty to import than a native and the distinction was soon made between those coming to trade and those coming to work. The latter evinced the wrath of the indigenous population who claimed that aliens would work for less and used their foreign 'mysteries' to undercut and outshine the established English trades and craftsmen. By the sixteenth century many of the expenses of the realm were financed or otherwise enabled by resident aliens to whom the law of the land proffered little protection or recourse. An alien, for example, had no right to own freehold property no matter how long he lived in England and upon his death, his fortune generally passed to the monarch, not to his heirs. When he paid taxes upon imports he paid at a higher rate than a native, sometimes twice as much; he was forbidden to sell by retail to certain classes of persons and excluded from practising many trades and professions except as an employee.

If the prosperity of the kingdom was to be maintained by the process of attracting foreign skills and capital to England then an amendment to the system was needed and so it came about that an alien was permitted to petition the monarch for Letters Patent of Denization which, when granted, would bestow upon him the status of 'denizen'. A denizen was still a foreigner but one recognised as a privileged class thereof, enjoying nearly as many rights as a native. The awarding to a foreigner of Letters Patent of Denization marked the beginning of a system of bureaucratic assimilation of aliens which in time would be simplified into the Naturalisation Acts of the eighteenth and nineteenth centuries.

Whilst England was discovering a way to either absorb or regulate the foreigners within its realm, its own subjects were venturing further and further afield in search of trading opportunities and the consequent wealth that this might bring. They were often travelling to lands with which their country enjoyed no form of diplomatic contact and in such circumstances, all they could do was to provide themselves with a documentary safeguard of some sort and hope that it would be honoured. In 1611, John Jourdain, an adventurer from Lyme Regis who had been engaged by the East India Company to open up trade in the Far East, travelled with a letter of introduction from King James I. In seeking contacts in India he was engaged in a race, for the Portuguese were already established on the west coast of India at Goa. After coming ashore and suffering several privations, not the least of which was being robbed of all his money and the letter from the king, Jourdain tried to regain the coast and found himself in the Kingdom of Jahangir. He applied for an audience with the king to secure a safe passage. As John Jourdain describes in his Journal, the King of Jahangir gave him a safe conduct although he opined that it was not really necessary within his peaceable kingdom.

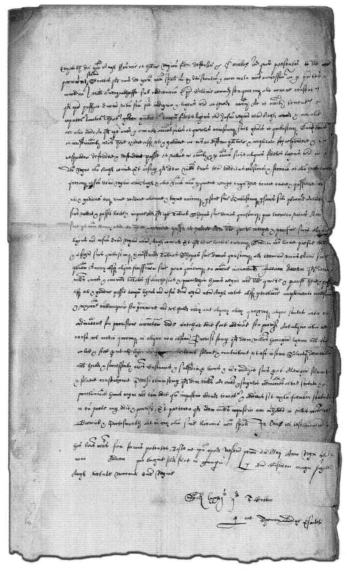

A warrant to issue Letters Patent of Denization to a citizen of
Cologne, William Grevynckhoffe, 'granted by our special grace,
certain knowledge and simple motion' by Queen Elizabeth I
on 1 May 1567. This document is written in Latin.

Soe at the daie appointed wee went, where as soone
as the Kinge came forth and was sett on his throne, he
called us to him, demandinge what our desire was. Wee
told him that wee had lost our shipp and that wee weare
desirious to travaile to gett home for our countrie by the
waye of Cambaia and Suratt; desiringe His Majestie that
hee would favour us with his passe as well for our quiett
travellinge as alsoe for the free passinge of our stuffe
without custome. He answered that his passe to travaile
was needlesse because his countrie was a free country for
all man, notwithstandinge wee should have his passe as
wee desired...[11]

At the end of the same decade, the Protestant Pilgrim
fathers set sail from England to establish themselves in His
Majesty's Plantations and Colonies in America. At this time
the settler population of the area which became the
thirteen original states was approximately 2,500; twenty
years later it was 25,000 and sixty years after that: 250,000.
The traffic was not all one way, there was a movement
between the Colonies and the Motherland and for this
passports were issued. A resident of England wishing to visit
America had to obtain a Licence from the Commissioners
for Plantations. The regulations for settlers were a little
more parochial. A colonist desirous of leaving Virginia
in the seventeenth century had to apply to the Governor for
a passport and this application was examined and approved
by the council and general court of the colony. A pass was
only issued after verification that the traveller had posted a
notice of his intended voyage on the church door for two
Sundays, and had settled all his debts.[12] Internal passports
were required for movement from one state to another and
this system survived until the revolutionary war. The
regulations for the issue of passports for overseas travel
were sent out from England under instruction of the Lords
of the Admiralty; the latter possibly saw such passports as a

natural extension to the well established use of ships' passports mentioned earlier.

There was not much point in requiring travellers to obtain passports if there existed no authority to check that they possessed them. At the beginning of the seventeenth century in England, Clerks of the Passage were introduced. Their job was to check whether travellers were properly documented. They were based at various ports around the kingdom and in the more important, such as Dover, they were overseen by a Commissioner. As the political tide of England ebbed and flowed so the focus of their attention was shifted. One of their early concerns was to prevent young men from embarking in order to become educated in the Catholic religion; St. Omer in northern France being a hotbed of Jesuits which attracted many adherents. They also compiled statistics on the numbers of people embarking for His Majesty's Plantations (America) and later, under Cromwell's rule, they regularly reported on the movements of agents of those wishing to restore the monarchy to the throne.

No system was infallible and the Clerks of the Passage could be bribed or simply duped. It was not unknown for disaffected parties to charter boats and embark from small creeks or even substantial ports with the connivance of the Clerks of the Passage who were there supposedly to prevent their very leaving.

In 1643, Sir Ralph Verney, a Member of Parliament seeking refuge in France obtained a pass in a particularly unimaginative false name thus:

To all Captaines and others whom it concerns
... These are to require you to permitt and suffer Mr. Ralph Smith and his wyffe and his man and mayde to passe by water to Lee in Essex and to returne. So they carry nothinge of Danger.
November the 30th. 1643 By warrant of the Ld. Maier...[13]

Sir Ralph embarked from the coast of Kent with the stated intention of crossing the river Thames from the southern bank to the northern, but once under sail, he then made all haste for the coast of France.

By the seventeenth century many European countries had the infrastructure to support an international passport system. The concept of the passport was recognised; there were educated scribes and clerks to issue the documents; there were civil and military authorities to check them. It was the passport itself that still needed to grow.

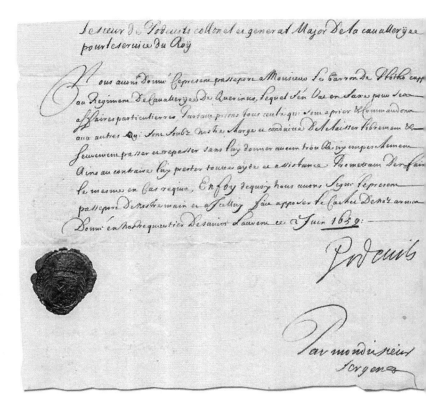

A passport to allow a German mercenary soldier in the pay of the French to return home during the War of the Pyrenees with Spain in 1659.

The document seen opposite is a passport issued in 1659 to enable an army officer to travel home during a war. The war in question was the dispute between France and Spain which broke out in the Pyrenees after the settlement of the Thirty Years War. It was not settled until November 1659 when the Treaty of the Pyrenees established once and for all the position of the frontier between the two countries. One of the ways in which the impoverished German princes would raise money was to sell mercenaries to any government that wanted them. It is possible that the Baron de Plotho, holder of this passport, was an officer in charge of some such mercenary force which had been leased to the service of King Louis XIV of France. The text is in French and translates as:

> The sire Poderits, colonel and major general of cavalry in the service of the King.
>
> We have given this present passport to Mr the Baron de Plotho, captain in the Querinus cavalry regiment, who is going to Saxony on private business we request of those who are to be requested and order the others who are under our influence and control to allow freely and surely to pass and repass without giving him any trouble or impediment even to the contrary to afford him all aid and assistance promising to do the same should the case arise. And for this we have signed the present passport with our own hand and had affixed to it the seal of our arms. Issued in our headquarters at Lauverne 2 June 1659.

We can only conjecture as to the nature of the private business which called the officer away. Perhaps he saw the end of the war approaching and pulled strings. It is fairly certain that with a return journey of over twelve hundred miles before him, the war would have been over before his return, if indeed he bothered to return.

The passport is handwritten by an orderly and then signed and sealed by the person under whose authority it is issued: Colonel Major-General Poderits. The document approximated to a convention in the content of its text but it obeyed no fixed rules or requirements in its size and layout. There is nothing to say that the next passport issued by the sire Poderits would resemble this document in any way. A uniform layout for a passport was only really possible once the state had established itself as the unique authority empowered to issue passports and in most countries, this was centuries away.

4

FLOG THE PEASANTS AGAIN

It was not unusual for the French Foreign Minister, Montmorin, to receive a letter from the Russian ambassador in Paris asking that he grant a passport. He had no reason to suspect that anything was amiss and so he acceded to Monsieur Simolin's request and issued a passport to replace the one that Madame de Korff asserted that she had mislaid:

By the Authority of the King

To all officers, civil and military charged with overseeing and maintaining public order in the different départements of the Kingdom and to all others similarly responsible, greeting. We order and direct that you allow to pass freely the Baron de Korff, going to Frankfurt with two children, a maid and a personal valet and three servants without giving him or allowing him to be given any obstruction. The present passport is valid for one month only.

Issued in Paris 5 June 1791[1]

He signed it 'Montmorin' with a flourish. That signature nearly cost him his life.

Less than two years earlier, in October 1789, King Louis XVI and Marie Antoinette had been brought forcibly into Paris from their palace in Versailles by the Paris revolutionary mob. They were at that very moment still under virtual house arrest a few hundred metres away in the Palace of the Tuileries. Powerless to affect the destiny of France and an embarrassment to the National Constituent Assembly government, they longed to imitate the actions of many of the aristocracy by fleeing to a friendly country. Now, thanks to Montmorin, they had an opportunity.

Using de Korff's passport, with Marie Antoinette posing as a maid and King Louis XVI as the personal valet, they left the Tuileries at night in a covered carriage and travelled eastwards towards Germany. A journey under the circumstances prevailing at that time was fraught not only with the usual inconveniences but also an additional danger. Unauthorised barriers had been thrown across roads and gangs of self-appointed officials would check carriages, their passengers and baggage with the twin purposes of hopefully discovering a fleeing monarchist sympathiser and enriching themselves into the bargain. A first-hand account of such an incident is contained in a contemporary letter from Mary Berry to Horace Walpole.

...The postilion on leaving Bourgoin stopped us at a corps de garde nationale where our passport was demanded which was one of the French Ambassador in London which had been signed by the mayor at Lyons. Our carriage was immediately surrounded by a number of people without uniforms or anything else to distinguish them who whilst they were examining our passport and asking eagerly if we were French people, told us they must search our trunks, "pas pour le contrabande mais pour les papiers".... Upon the officers coming out again and telling them that our passport was a perfectly good one, that they saw or rather heard that we were English and that having searched our trunk they need not look further we were allowed to proceed, the officer having put upon our passport "vu et fouillé" which he said would prevent our being searched again at the pont de Beauvoisin. I really began to dread being searched at every village...[2]

The royal fugitives had less to fear than most since, according to their papers, they were unnamed servants travelling for their foreign masters, the Korffs. Was it this very feeling of security that prompted the King to poke his head out of the carriage window or was it a desire to take a last look at France? We shall never know but the consequences were disastrous. A retired soldier called Deurne recognised the King's face as the carriage rattled by. He hurriedly saddled his horse and set off to follow them. When the carriage reached the small town of Varennes en Argonne about 15 miles from the border with the Austrian Netherlands, they stopped to take fresh horses. Deurne galloped ahead, his military training coming through, for he was intent on securing the bridge on the River Aire which lay a further two kilometres past the town and over which the royal party would have to pass. He persuaded the keepers to close the barrier and then galloped back and roused the town.

The prisoners were taken from the carriage to the town hall where they were held until the following day by which time a troop of guards had arrived from Paris to escort them back. For Louis XVI it was the ultimate irony of identification. Travelling in disguise in a time before the existence of identity photographs, he had been recognised from the likeness of his head which was engraved on the *assignats*, a form of promissory note, of the epoch.

On hearing of the incident the public was incensed and demanded the punishment of any person implicated in assisting the royals' escape. It became known that the foreign minister, Montmorin, had issued the passport and they howled for his blood. A guard of four gendarmes was assigned to protect his life and property whilst an inquiry was instigated. Fortunately for him, in his department's file was found the letter from Madame de Korff claiming, falsely as it had turned out, that she had lost her first passport and requesting a replacement. This exculpated him but Louis XVI and Marie Antoinette were not so fortunate. They were returned to captivity and their ultimate fate.

When the new French Republic was proclaimed in 1792, Liberty, Equality and Fraternity were the maxims of the day and so passports and all similar controls were swept away as being contrary to the ideas of freedom implicit in the revolution. The decrees of 1623 and 1669 declaring that nobody was allowed to leave the kingdom of Louis XIV without a passport were abolished; the rules which had been introduced for internal regulation of the population were removed. These had been used to control the movement of peasants from the country to the towns, to prevent capital and skills from moving out of specific geographical areas and to return destitute paupers to the parishes where they were born.

It was soon realised that Liberty should not be an absolute but rather a gradeable concept. Lawlessness increased alarmingly throughout the land. The brigands and other criminals having been relieved of the necessity of acquiring documents for travel from one town to another were now untrackable by the police. A result of the civil unrest was that those of the population who could afford to, emigrated to escape its worst effects and in doing so, of course, were able to take their capital with them since there were no passport laws to prevent them. France, already teetering on the verge of bankruptcy, saw financial doom staring it in the face. It did the only thing it could. It reintroduced the passport requirement for internal and external travel. The document seen opposite is one such passport, issued in 1795 and requiring five signatures:

Liberty, Equality, Fraternity, Unity, Humanity.
    No 566
Department of Orne, District of Domfront, Commune of Athis, Head Town of the Canton.
Allow to pass freely, the citizen Robert Planchon, cultivator,

passport
ued in
volutionary
ance to Robert
anchon,
armhand,
1795.

required five
natures and
is described
wn to the
our of his
ebrows and
e shape
his nose.

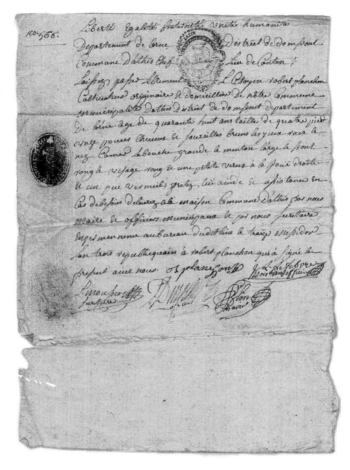

originating from and living in our commune, Municipality of
Athis, District of Domfront, Department of Orne, aged forty
eight years height four feet eleven inches brown hair and
eyebrows brown eyes flat nose large mouth wide chin round
forehead round face with a small spot on the right cheek and
going a bit grey give him help and assistance in case of need.
Issued at the Town Hall of Athis by us the Mayor and
municipal officers and by us the Secretary at the office of the
aforementioned town the thirteenth Messidor in the third
year of the Republic to Robert Planchon who has signed the
present with us.

Note that the passport was issued at an early time in the revolutionary period and the new calendar has been used, 'the thirteenth Messidor', however, the holder's height is still measured in feet and inches (*'pieds'* and *'pouces'*) because the metric system would not be introduced for another two years.

The persecution of the aristocracy had resulted inevitably in a massive flight from France to countries such as the Rhineland and Switzerland from where the refugees could view developments in France with a view to choosing the best moment to return. These populations of *émigrés* as they were known, caused considerable trouble for the receiving countries not only because of their numbers but also because of the pressure which the French revolutionary government brought to bear upon the host countries.

In July 1795 the Rt Hon William Wickham was named the British Minister Plenipotentiary to the Swiss Cantons and the Grisons. In a letter to his German counterpart in the following June, he expressed regret at the decision of the Swiss Cantons to submit to the demands of France as represented by François Barthélemy.

> Your Excellency will learn doubtless with pain or rather indignation that this Canton which was formerly so proud of its independence decided in a full meeting of the Council yesterday to submit to the request of Monsieur Barthélemy to expel the Emigrés. I do not know what your Excellency would consider the best course of action on this occasion but for my part, I will certainly not grant them passports to go to England except in a few exceptional circumstances...[3]

Wickham wrote to his master, Lord Grenville, in London, regrettably informing him of the Swiss Council of 200's decision to comply with Mr Barthélemy's request before the 1 August and estimating that as a result, of the 5,000 estimated *émigrés* in Switzerland, 800 to 1,000 might want to come to England. He confirmed that he had not yet issued passports and awaited instructions to this effect.

The use of passports as a means of control in Europe was exploited ruthlessly by Napoleon I. He used armies and threats to coerce nations, and passports to intimidate individuals. The vivacious Madame De Stael, the daughter of the former finance minister of Louis XVI, Jacques Necker, incurred Napoleon's displeasure by the success of her political writings which tended towards liberalism. She was witty and outspoken and showed much courage in sustaining her beliefs in the face of Napoleon's obsessive persecution of her. He had her banished from within 40 leagues of Paris. This was a bitter blow to a lady who flourished on the life of the literary salon but she was to learn just how far Napoleon could make his influence felt when she began her trip to Russia in her attempt to reach Sweden. Arriving in Poland, she intended to stay a few days with some acquaintances in the local chateau.

> My carriage stopped before the customs post and my son, as usual, went to get my passport stamped. At the end of a quarter of an hour I was surprised that he had not returned and asked M Schlegel to find out what was causing the delay... My son, beside himself, informed me that the police chief had told him that I could not stay longer than eight hours and to ensure that I obeyed this order, one of his commissaires would follow me to the chateau, go in with me and would only leave me after my departure... [4]

This hounding of Madame de Stael also extended to her family and friends. Her English companion, Fanny Randall, tried to get a passport from the local police to enable her to proceed to Paris and thence to Geneva where Madame de Stael was living. The police refused because she was English so she returned another day and pretended to have been born in Switzerland and was given a passport for Paris. Once in Paris she was again refused a passport for Geneva

Joseph Fouché 1763-1820.

As Minister of Police and then Minister of the Interior under four French administrations, Fouché used the Passport System as a tool of pitiless State repression and control.

so she demanded an audience with the Chief of Police, Fouché. He listened attentively to her pleas and her assurance that the only reason she wished to go to Geneva was to visit her sister and then he smugly produced the letter she had written to Madame de Stael which proved the contrary. He arrogantly informed her that she would never get a passport. But Fouché had underestimated the resourcefulness of the Englishwoman. She befriended an Irish clerk whom she had noticed working in his office. He wrote out a passport for her, pushed it in amongst some routine military papers and got it signed by the Minister of War and with that document she travelled to Geneva.[5]

The rigour and fanatacism with which Fouché carried out his duties as Minister of Police in Paris from July 1799 onwards were to make him a symbol of repression and an example of all that was wrong in Europe with the Passport System. His dogged inflexibility with regard to duty could occasionally appear misguided to the point of folly. When Napoleon Bonaparte left his army in Egypt and returned hurriedly to France in October 1799 to seize power, Fouché remarked that by landing at Fréjus and travelling directly to Paris, Bonaparte had violated the quarantine laws which had been put there to protect the health of the nation.

Although the first French Republic from which Napoleon seized power was a new government and a new idea, it was not a new country. The forms and procedures necessary for diplomatic relations and the issue and recognition of passports which were already in existence could be adapted. Just before the declaration of the French Republic, however, a new nation had been invented: the United States of America, formed by the breaking away from Great Britain of the former Plantations, Colonies and other territories annexed or won by conquest in the New World. The American War of Independence was over by 1781, victory having been assisted in no uncertain degree by the naval contribution of the French. The preliminary Treaty of Peace was signed in 1782 in Paris and a United States Department of Foreign Affairs, later to become the Department of State, was given the job of issuing passports. The first US Legation was established in 1777 and by 1780 some of the US passports issued in Paris and London already bore descriptions of their holders and a stated duration of validity, usually three or six months.

One could imagine that if a country had just invented itself then it could indulge in all manner of innovations and peculiarities in designing its passport and not feel bound by centuries of tradition but a passport requires certain basic elements in order to function. The US Minister

Passport of Stephen L Serlate. 'he demeaning himself well and peaceably' issued by the Mayor of New York on 'the second day of May in the year of our Lord one thousand eight hundred and twenty five and of the Independence of the United States, the forty ninth'.

Plenipotentiary in Paris, Benjamin Franklin, in designing the American passport to be issued at his Legation, found a practical solution to avoid too much head-scratching. He took the contemporary French passport and modelled the text of his new passports upon it. He then printed them upon his own press at his house in Passy, Paris.[6]

Although the Department of Foreign Affairs was the countrywide authority to issue American passports this did not stop the Governors of the individual American states from still issuing their own passports and so travellers could now choose to equip themselves with a passport issued for foreign travel by the state or city in which they were resident or one of the new 'Departmental Passports' as they were called.

The nineteenth century opened to find a Europe reeling from the effects of one revolution and ignorant of the intensifying influence of another. On the academic front the French Revolution had brought into common consciousness the concept of nationality, and the outflux of refugees fleeing the physical terrors and excesses of the revolution had evinced a reaction in Great Britain in 1793 in the form of the first Aliens Act whose preamble declared that, '...much Danger may arise to the publick Tranquillity from the Resort and Residence of Aliens unless due Provision be made in respect thereof...'[7]

Further acts followed and the restrictions were altered and compounded as the tide of peace and war ebbed and flowed. Such measures were workable because passports existed. When a more lasting peace became certain after Napoleon's defeat at Waterloo, the requirements were eased somewhat.

But it was the Industrial Revolution which was to cause countries to rethink their passport requirements. A new class was growing in the social order, the middle class, whose wealth was derived from trade and industry and this class, particularly in Great Britain, had the money and the inclination to travel abroad. The passport which had evolved from a sort of cross fertilisation of the King's Licence and the letter of introduction was no longer a privilege granted to the most noble, it had become an administrative document demanded by many and a proper bureaucracy was required to meet the demand.

The railways spread their tentacles far and wide and long-distance travel for the working classes became cheap and quick. On the Continent, this phenomenal increase in the numbers of individuals moving about the land made the running of an internal police system based on passports, ludicrously unworkable. The profusion of documents of differing values of credibility, being checked by control regimes of equally varied efficiency in a continent which, despite its achievements in the field of intellect, still boasted pockets of ignorance and feudalism, sometimes produced unfortunate results.

Consider the experience of Mr Hill, the British Vice-Consul in Fiume. Disgruntled but not overly surprised at being summoned in the middle of a June night in 1837 he stumbled into his boots and went downstairs to see what all the fuss was about.

In 1837 Fiume, now Rijeka in Croatia, was a flourishing port of the Austro-Hungarian Empire. Through its three harbours on the Adriatic Sea passed the wine, figs and other fruit of Hungary. Its town boasted a castle, many fine churches and convents, and latterly, a sugar refinery and wax manufactory. The streets teemed with a hotch-potch of Serbs, Hungarians, Italians and Croats. The presence of a British Vice Consul was necessary to look after the interests of the local British community engaged in shipping and exporting. Whilst the town itself might have presented the image of a cosmopolitan and sophisticated settlement, Mr Hill knew, as he rode the eighteen miles inland into the night-darkened hills, that he was returning to the Middle Ages.

An Englishman had got himself into trouble with some villagers. In truth, the trouble was not of his doing but was a product of the meeting of the administrative ethos of nineteenth-century Europe and the ingrained prejudices of an uneducated peasantry. Upon being shown to the village headman's house, the Vice-Consul was outraged to find the

Englishman wounded and in chains, and an inquisition in progress. He demanded the man's immediate release and that an explanation be provided. The judge of the peasants, along with the Catholic priest, objected to the Englishman's passport saying that it was a forgery. It was a splendid British passport, sporting an impressive coat of arms. Unfortunately, it had been issued shortly after the sudden death of King William IV and so the pre-printed form had been amended by the crossing out of any mention of the King and the substitution of the name of the new monarch, Queen Victoria.

Mr Hill patiently explained this to the judge but he was not mollified for the bearer was described as a lieutenant-colonel.

> 'And why not?' said Mr Hill.
> 'Well,' answered the judge, 'he may be a lieutenant colonel, but a little way further on he is described as a gentleman! What can you say to that?'[8]

No doubt suppressing as much irony as he could, the Vice-Consul explained that in England, being an officer in the Army did not exclude one from also being a gentleman. Hoping that he had at last satisfied the man of religion he made to depart but was prevented by a further objection. The priest shoved the Englishman's visiting card under the Vice-Consul's nose. This showed his title as 'reverend'. When the Vice-Consul explained that the man had taken holy orders upon retirement from the Army, the priest silently pointed to the man's travelling companion – his fourteen-year-old son. That an army officer could possibly be also considered as a gentleman was just believable to a Catholic priest but that a priest should have a son utterly outside his comprehension.

At length the force of argument of the Vice-Consul prevailed and the man was freed. When Mr Hill warned the priest and head of the village that he was going to submit a complaint to the authorities they tried to appease him – they led him to the window and showed him the peasants being flogged for having assaulted the man. Mr Hill and his charges hurriedly took their leave and, true to his word, the Vice-Consul submitted a strongly worded report through the official channels. He pointed out that it was the officials who had conducted the trial who should have been punished, not the peasants. After a delay of eleven months, possibly exacerbated by the confusion over whether Fiume was part of Hungary or the Kingdom of Croatia, the Austrian civil service responded magnificently by leaving the officials in office and having the peasants flogged again.

The bureaucracy of travel was conspued by the new class of traveller for whom it was an irritation and inconvenience to be either suffered or overcome.

In the middle of the nineteenth century, a publisher called John Gadsby set off towards the Mediterranean and North Africa with a view to improving his health. For the entertainment of his friends, he compiled a detailed account of his experiences. This was a time when one's national reputation was just as influential as one's passport. Upon arriving in Constantinople he recounts, 'I went to look after my passport. The office was closed but as soon as I had made it known that I was an Englishman the door was opened and my passport viséd. One of the clerks spoke English well and was very kind to me.'[10]

He candidly recognised the twin advantages of being English and of England not having an internal passport control on his observations of:

> ...a Maltese who had been in the service of our consul at Jerusalem. He had come with a party from Jerusalem to Cairo intending then to go to Malta by way of Alexandria but when he reached that port, as he had left his passport at Jerusalem, the officers sent him back to Cairo whence he would have to go again to Jerusalem. This was no joke but such is the

passport system. Had it occurred in Austria or Russia he would not have got off so easily but would have been sent to prison for travelling without a passport or permit. What would we English say if we could not go from London to the Crystal Palace or from Manchester to Stockport without a passport or a police officer at our heels? Depend upon it, we are not half enough grateful to God for our national privileges.[11]

In Gadsby's dealings with the ignorance or corruption of foreign officialdom he adopted a mixture of guile and scorn.

On my second visit to Rome the officers told us we must all go into the police office as one of our passports was missing. My companion who spoke Italian fluently, endeavoured to convince them they were in error, but it was all to no purpose. They were certain they were right. At last I recollected myself and said 'Oh I know all about it!' I stepped into the office and gave the senior officer two francs when, quick as thought about, he discovered that he had accidentally overlooked the missing passport and we were speedily on our way.[12]

And in the Milan of Austro-Hungaria:

We sent our passports to the police office and were told they were all right but we must appear at the office as the superintendent wished to see 'what we were like'. Of course we went because we could not help ourselves.
'Were you ever in Milan before?'
'Never.'
'What is the object of your visit?'
'Health and recreation.'
'When do you think of leaving?'
'As soon as ever we can get away.'
Our guide, however, turned pale and durst not interpret the last answer but said 'Mattino'. The functionary bowed, my companion bowed, I bowed, our guide cringed and we withdrew.[13]

Travel in the nineteenth century was not as comfortable as it is today. Contemporary print showing passengers on board a Channel Packet.

Gadsby's account tells us as much about the Victorian traveller as it does of the countries he visited. The insular British suddenly finding themselves able to meet the foreigner on his home ground tended to treat him with scorn and as an inferior. The writer Charles Dickens spent many months of his life travelling and living abroad and his letters often showed a different point of view. When he considered the rudeness and repression that was perceived in foreign officials by the British tourist he observed that it was a product of the latter's own doing. 'I am strongly inclined to think that our countrymen are to blame in the matter of the Austrian vexations to travellers that have been complained of.' He believed that the manner in which the Englishman behaved abroad was such that it invited an officious reaction. 'They are so extraordinarily suspicious, so determined to be done by everybody, and give so much offence.' He agreed that the Austrian police were very strict but he admired their efficiency and politeness: 'if you treat them like gentlemen, they will always respond.' His dealings with the officials were most cordial: 'When we first crossed the Austrian frontier, and were ushered into the police office, I took off my hat. The officer immediately took off his and was as polite – still doing his duty – as it was possible to be.'[14]

In 1853, when coming in to Venice by train he recounts the scene: 'A soldier has come into the railway carriage... has touched his hat and asked for my passport. I have given it. Soldier has touched his hat again, and retired as from the presence of a superior officer. Alighted from carriage, we pass into a place like a banking-house, lighted up with gas. Nobody bullies us or drives us there but we must go because the road ends there... My passport is brought out of an inner room, certified to be en règle. Very sharp chief takes it, looks at it (it is rather longer now than Hamlet) calls out – "Signor Carlo Dickens!" The thing being done at all, could not be better done or more politely.'[15]

However, even Dickens could not resist enjoying some good-natured fun at the expense of the passport office procedure at Boulogne. In a letter to his friend John Forster who was intending to visit him in Paris in 1846, he prepares him for the ordeal:

> You are filtered into the little office, where there are some soldiers and a gentleman with a black beard and a pen and ink sitting behind a counter.
> Black Beard: 'Your passport monsieur!'
> Monsieur: 'Here it is monsieur.'
> Black Beard: 'Where are you going monsieur?'
> Monsieur: 'I am going to Paris monsieur.'
> Black Beard: 'When are you leaving monsieur?'
> Monsieur: 'I am leaving today, monsieur, on the mail coach.'
> Black Beard: 'That's fine. *(to the Gendarme)* Allow the monsieur to pass.'
> Gendarme: 'This way monsieur.'[16]

In Egypt, Gadsby crossed swords with a nationality that was already beginning to display the qualities which would, in the next century, carry it on to supplant the British as the most eagerly awaited tourists.

During a squabble between native servants, pistols were drawn and the Governor of the town was called in to mediate. 'I now took out my passport to which I had had attached the Turkish Seal at Constantinople, and showing it to the Governor, I desired the dragoman to say that if he did not protect us come what may we would go back to Cairo and report him to the Pasha...' To Gadsby's obvious annoyance, his American companion stepped up to him and, '...peremptorily demanded that I should take it away. "What good" said he, "can an English passport do here?" "Well," I replied, "try yours if you think it will answer better".'[14] The matter was resolved eventually but not without Gadsby relieving his pique by adding a footnote to his account: 'There are three classes of person with whom no man ought to travel, unless he is prepared to submit to many annoyances: 1) Young conceited officers in the army, 2) Half-educated schoolmasters and 3) American slaveowners.'[17]

The question of the credibility of the American passport was one which had worried the United States Department of State for some time for the individual American states had continued to issue their own passports. The control over the issue of these was very slack; town mayors and even notaries public would issue passports. Sometimes a stock of passport forms would be issued to an official with the sole instruction that he satisfy himself that the applicant was American before issuing, with no indication or guidelines as to how he was supposed to do it.

Overseas travel degenerated into the ludicrous situation wherein Americans travelling on passports issued by their local state would discover that European countries would not recognise them unless they had been subsequently endorsed by the US Legation in that country. Those who held Departmental Passports had no such problem.

To remedy this situation, in 1856 the USA passed a law which made the Department of State the sole authority for issuing American passports. The law also brought an unwelcome innovation – a fee of $1 for a passport valid for overseas travel. Up until then, all passports had been issued gratis. By the same act, the officers issuing such passports were warned that to issue a passport to a non-American could result in a fine or even, loss of office.

The Passport System as practised in nineteenth-century Europe was not the only system in the world which involved tokens of permission and identity; it became the most widespread because of the success of the colonising efforts of the major European powers. Great tracts of Africa, Asia, America and all of Australasia were governed by peoples of European stock and they naturally brought with them the administrative system of their mother countries.

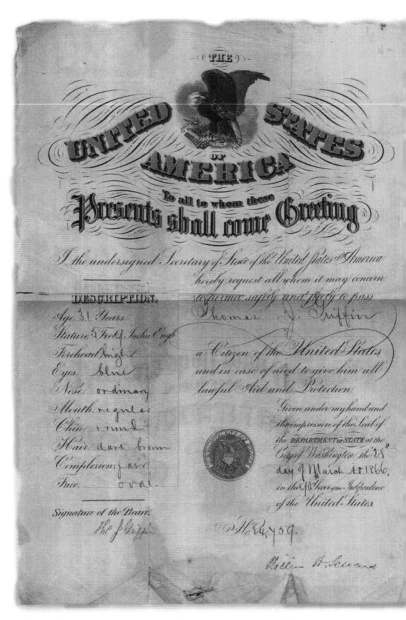

A 'departmental passport' of the USA, issued by the
Department of State in Washington in 1866 for a fee of $6.

In the Far East, the empires of China and Japan showed little interest in exploration or colonisation. Apart from Buddhist pilgrimages to India in the early fifth century and the voyages of Cheng Ho in the fifteenth, the Chinese seemed rarely to have ventured outside their world. They had little need to establish a passport system for travelling overseas and no colonies upon whom to impose such a structure. Both China and Japan, however, operated an internal control which required permissions for travel to be demanded from local lords. As with all these systems, they were designed mainly to control a working population for the greater economic benefit of the ruling class.

In the early seventeenth century, Japan had courted English, Dutch, Portuguese and Spanish traders who were permitted to set up trading bases known as 'factories', but the Europeans amazed and disturbed the Japanese by the barbarity and jealousy with which they conducted their operations and so in 1641, by an order of the shogun Iyenitsu, Europeans were banned. Five years earlier he had made an order forbidding the Japanese to leave the islands and this isolation from all foreign influence prevailed until the American Commodore Perry steamed into Uraga harbour in 1853 with orders from his government to reopen Japan to trade.

The earliest Japanese passports issued were 'Licences to Travel Overseas' and date from the end of the Edo period 1866-68. Because of the stamp impression on the front of these documents they were invariably called 'seals' and the name 'passport seal' stuck with the Japanese passport until the end of the Second World War. The passports were manufactured of one sheet of thick paper roughly 12in x 8$\frac{1}{2}$in with the text on the front in Japanese and on the verso in English. The personal description distinguished itself from the European equivalent by including an observation not on the 'colour of eyes' but 'size of eyes'.

The Chinese had continued to trade with Europeans by restricting their movements and activities to certain ports and towns. So successful were they with their trade that they began to gather considerable wealth partly because of the Europe-wide desirability of their exports and partly because of their remarkable self-sufficiency in many areas. But they too had to succumb to the greed-induced aggression of Europe. In 1842, Britain, responding to China's attempt to stop it from supplying Indian opium to its subjects, marched a military force up the Yangtse and forced China to sign the Treaty of Nanking. Hostilities continued intermittently between various European nations and China for the following twenty years.

By the end of the nineteenth century, access to China and Japan was by means of the Treaty Ports, within the

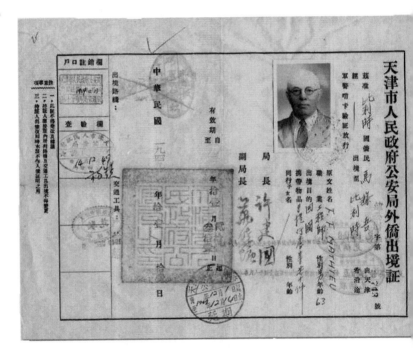

A permit for a foreigner to leave China by ship via Tientsin in 1949.

confines of which, foreigners did not need passports. For any voyage to the interior, however, a passport was needed.

The indomitable cyclist, J. Foster Fraser, who in 1899 along with two companions completed a 19,000 mile circumnavigation of the earth by bicycle, discovered that the local mandarin was ignorant of the existence of the Treaty of Pekin of 1897. When finally the passports were issued, their being the first issued to British subjects entering China from Burma, he found them to be: '...of enormous size, of coarse paper covered with wonderful marks in black and red and the three of them would easily paper the walls of an ordinary London hotel bedroom. One side of each passport was in Chinese and the other side contained a very free translation in English.'[18]

His passport began: 'I, the Prefect Wun, Wearer of the Peacock's Feather by grant of the Emperor and holding Permanent Office in the Prefecture of the Kingdom, and acting as Prefect of Teng-Yueh, Do Hereby grant a passport to John Foster Fraser...'[19]

In the case of Japan, to obtain a passport to travel inland in the 1890s, the traveller had to apply to his own consulate who would in turn apply to the Japanese authorities. For this service the British Legation charged its subjects two dollars whereas the American Consulate charged theirs a few cents. The intended route had to be stated in the application because this was entered on the passport and checked at each major town through which the traveller passed. For those travellers unversed in Oriental geography the British Legation had concocted a series of set routes from which one could choose.

Despite the apparent severity of this control, in practice it could be quite lax. It was generally accepted that one could visit Tokyo without a passport despite its not being a Treaty Port and one or two of the Japanese provinces would sometimes issue a passport with no objection raised whatsoever.[18]

By now the passport had begun to adapt to the needs of contemporary travel. Still either a single sheet or a double folded sheet, it was a pre-printed form onto which an issuing officer entered the details of the bearer in manuscript. It would often bear a fiscal stamp which was

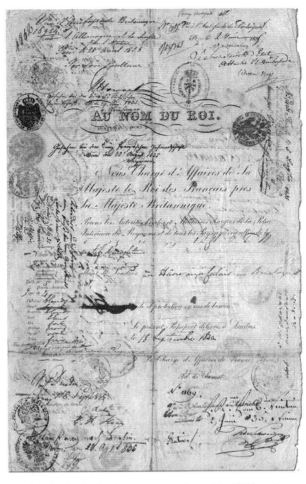

A French single sheet passport issued in 1835 and utterly obscured by the visas and frontier stamps applied on its first journey.

nothing other than a tax with the revenue raised going straight into the coffers of the issuing government. As we have seen from Orsini's case, although the Continental and American passports required the bearer to be described physically, the British passport bore no description all through the nineteenth century and it was only in the first decade of the twentieth century that two descriptive details were added: age, expressed in years, and occupation.

The single sheet was practical in that it took up little space in the traveller's pocket book in which he kept his money. If it was only used for one short journey then it was sufficient for its purpose but as people began to travel more regularly and use their passports several times, then the danger arose that the document could be obscured by the many endorsements made for visas and currency controls. For example, before the unification of Italy in 1861 and Germany in 1871, every Italian duchy and German

The British passport of Charles Saward, 1878.
His application was recommended by the
Bank of England but submittted to the
Foreign Office by an agent who then bound
the single sheet into a leather wallet.

kingdom issued its own visas. This meant that the administrative requirements of a journey through Europe could obliterate a passport.

A solution to this problem was found by the passport agents whose livelihood was assured by relieving intending travellers of the burden of filling in and submitting the passport application forms. They would often supply the document neatly folded into a little leather wallet, complete with a notebook meant for the observations of the traveller on the road, or the recording of important memoranda such as train departure times. This notebook provided many blank pages and the consulates were quick to appropriate them and thereupon affix their visas. In this manner the single-sheet passport grew an unofficial annexe.

And from that modification it should have been only a short step to making a passport completely in booklet form but there was another, more striking innovation to be adopted first.

5

IT DOESN'T LOOK A BIT LIKE ME

Charles A. Inglis never received his passport back. Germany declared war on Russia on 1 August 1914 and immediately the US Embassy in Berlin was besieged by hundreds of American citizens demanding the passports that they had not needed until then. All the embassy employees were called in to work, along with any volunteers that could be found. Even an eleven-year-old girl who was a house guest of the Ambassador was roped in. The chaos was indescribable with Americans who had been rendered destitute by the refusal of the banks to honour their letters of credit, queuing upstairs in the ballroom to obtain places on the special evacuation trains which were being run from Berlin through to Holland and Denmark. It should not be surprising that in the midst of this turmoil, Inglis' passport should go astray. What is surprising is the manner of its disappearance.

In order to leave Germany, all Americans had to submit their passports to the German Foreign Ministry at 76 Willhelmstrasse to have an exit permit endorsed therein. When enquiries were made as to the whereabouts of Inglis' passport, the Foreign Ministry replied that it had been collected by somebody from the United States Embassy. This was not the truth.

On 27 August, an American named Charles A. Inglis registered at the North British Hotel in Edinburgh, Scotland. He spent a few days sightseeing and on 30th he sent a telegram to Stockholm from the Edinburgh General Post Office. The counter clerk, William Mills, remembered insisting that he add the surname 'Inglis' to his signature 'Charles' on the telegram. On September 1, he checked out of the hotel, instructing them to forward his mail to the Cunard Company in Liverpool, and he rented lodgings with a Mrs Brown in the city. He said he was an American tourist whose holidays had been interrupted by the war and was now having difficulty in getting home. He hired a bicycle and visited the countryside around Queen's Ferry and the Rosyth Naval Base. A fortnight later, Charles A. Inglis could be found at the Ivanhoe Hotel in London, visiting the capital as any tourist would.

Inglis then passed through Liverpool en route to Holyhead, a port from which ships departed for Ireland. There he showed his American passport to Mr Hussey, the Aliens Officer and embarked. He met another American on the boat and they decided to go together to the Gresham Hotel in Dublin.

Two or three days later, Inglis was sitting in the lounge of the Great Southern Hotel in Killarney when there was a page-call put out for Mr Charles Inglis. He made himself known to a serious looking individual who, after confirming his identity with a Stanleyan, 'Mr Inglis I presume?' introduced himself as District Inspector Cheeseman of the Royal Irish Constabulary and requested to be shown to his bedroom. Once there, D.I. Cheeseman came straight to the point.

'I arrest you as a suspected German agent.'
'What is this? Me a German agent? Take care, I am an American citizen.'[1]

Despite his protestation he was taken to Killarney police barracks and searched. Apart from his passport and a quantity of English, German and Norwegian money, his notebook contained along with various accounts of his travel expenditure, notes of British and German naval losses and some addresses in Berlin, Bergen and Hamburg. The innocence of the latter, Inglis might have been able to explain were it not for the fact that the letters that he had mailed to these addresses had already been opened and read by the British authorities.

He was brought under guard to London and imprisoned in Wellington Barracks, close to Buckingham Palace. On 30 October 1914, he was summoned to a court martial at the Middlesex Guildhall, charged with espionage.

It transpired that the man arrested as Charles A. Inglis was actually a German called Carl Hans Lody who had polished his command of English whilst working under Norwegian, British and American flags in the Mercantile Marine. For several years he had travelled between America and Europe.

In 1900 Lody had entered the German Navy, served for a year and then had been put on the General Reserve. After this he had found employment with the Hamburg Amerika Shipping Line as a tourist agent and travelled a considerable amount. In 1910 passengers on the Hamburg Amerika Steamship *Cleveland* remembered him as being intelligent, quick-witted and attractive to the ladies. Miss Stors, the daughter of a wealthy Omaha brewer, had presumably thought so too since, after meeting him when on a tour of Germany and Europe, she married him in 1912. The marriage, however, was not a success and they were divorced a few months later. Lody was recompensed by his ex-wife's father to the tune of $10,000 and he then returned to Germany.

At his trial Lody said that when in Berlin in 1913 he had made representations to the General Department of the Navy to be taken from the active service list because he knew that he could no longer be a seaman – his eyesight was failing and he had been left physically weakened by the removal of two ribs during an operation for an internal abscess. His desire was to return to the USA where he still had many former business and social contacts.

Unfortunately, the German Navy had other ideas for him. It was known that he had travelled widely and was generally taken for an American. He was asked to go to England by a man whom he would only describe as a superior officer, and report back on the losses of the Royal Navy after their first confrontation with the German Navy. Then he was to travel about and take in anything of use that he could as a tourist he was told not to spy since his real job would await him in America. His reaction was one of reluctance and uncertainty. 'I felt I was not a fit man for a job of that kind. I was so well known to many people and so accustomed to be called by my own name that I felt that I would make a blunder with the first man I met.'[2] When he pointed out that in any case, he would need proper papers he was given an American passport in the name of Charles A. Inglis. Lody then went to Hamburg where his passport was viséd by the United States Consul to allow him to return to the USA. Four days later he was in Norway and within the week, in Scotland.

The court martial lasted for three days and was not without its irony and excitement. At the first hearing, one of the witnesses, the elderly Mrs Brown who had rented him a room in Edinburgh, was asked if she could see the accused in the court. She immediately began to scrutinise closely the members of the court martial. Lody let her out of her embarrassment by waving to her. And on the second day a young man 'of foreign appearance' who had gained admission on both days by showing naval papers was pounced upon, questioned and searched and then marched off under armed guard to Wellington Barracks.

Parts of the court martial were held in camera due to the sensitivity of the disclosures but it was stated that the letters he had mailed to Norway had been intercepted by a special section of the Post Office set up for that purpose at the beginning of hostilities. In each envelope was found a further sealed letter to be posted to Berlin and when these were opened they gave accurate details of British warships and their armaments and warned that important buildings such as the Houses of Parliament were protected from Zeppelin attack by strong wire mesh netting. Lody refused to divulge the name of his senior officer because he had given his word not to but he made no attempt to deny that he was a spy. Curiously, one of the letters to Norway he had signed in the code name, 'Nazi'.

Lody was found guilty on 2 November and taken to Wellington Barracks. During the night of 11 November he was taken from there to the Tower for execution. Just before daybreak he was brought out before the firing squad on the miniature rifle range in the Tower of London. He turned to the officer in charge of the firing squad and said, 'I suppose you won't shake the hand of a spy' and the officer replied, 'I will always shake the hand of a brave man,'[3] and did so. He was then put on a chair, the officer gave the order and eight rifles fired. The news of the execution was not officially released for four days but workers who slept in the Tower had been awoken by the volley and guessed its import; in hushed voices they whispered the news to the various visitors to the Tower.

This was the first execution for espionage in the Tower of London since 1700 and did not pass without controversy. The *New York Times* in its editorial observed that despite the fact that Lody was no doubt guilty, the British had missed an opportunity to ignore the standard penalty and in executing him they would surely make him a martyr. It was well known, they opined, that the threat of execution would never stop spies from spying. Perhaps they thought that the fear of obscurity would. Lody's remains were buried within the confines of the Tower but were later removed to a pauper's grave.

Was it unrealistic for the German authorities to believe that Lody could succeed in impersonating an American? Not at all. He had lived for some years in the USA and spoke the language in the correct idiom and of course his identity was corroborated by a genuinely issued American passport which required no falsification, for the American passport of the day was a single-sheet document, valid for two years and which did not bear a photograph. When Lody said that he was Charles A. Inglis, who was to deny it?

On 21 December 1914, five weeks after Lody's death, the United States Secretary of State, William Jennings Bryan introduced the requirement for all new passports issued to bear a photograph of the holder. The principle of photography had been known for over a hundred years, why had it taken so long for it to reach passports?

One important factor in the delay was its feasibility. The first of the practical photographic processes was developed by the Frenchman Daguerre in consort with Niepce and was made public in 1839. It required a copper plate to be coated with pure silver oxide and exposed to the light for a long period. The daguerrotype as it was called was quickly exploited in other countries and manufacturers were not slow to offer for sale the means to master this new process. An apparatus for making a daguerrotype which would consist of a camera with a lens, silvered plates and chemicals was soon put on sale at about 400 francs (roughly £16) but the portrait itself could be sold for anything from 60 to 120 francs (£2.40 to £4.80). Whilst competition very quickly reduced the costs, it did little initially to improve the quality of the lens which was still what one would classify as 'slow'.

In 1839 the first portrait exposure, as opposed to landscape where nothing moves, was made in the USA and required the sitter to remain motionless for 30 minutes facing the sunlight. As with many new technologies, the greatest improvements were seen in the early years. In the following year, exposure time for a portrait photograph was one minute and the price was $5. It was discovered that by mixing bromine with the silver nitrate coating it was possible to reduce the exposure time to one second. This now made the whole process far less onerous and far more attractive to the public and by 1841, portrait studios were in existence Europe-wide. Further improvements came in the matter of coatings and in lenses designed specifically with the optimum focal lengths to ensure sharpness for portraits.

Throughout the latter half of the nineteenth century many trials were conducted with a view to discovering a suitable film medium but before these came to commercial fruition, photography was given a boost by the development of the glass negative and the craze for *carte de visite* type photographs.

The notion of having a photograph of oneself pasted to one's visiting card was probably the idea of several people simultaneously in the 1850s. In practice the cards could not have been very successful as visiting cards, bearing on the verso as they usually did, the name and address of the photographer. In Continental Europe the fad was led by a fashionable French photographer, André Adolphe Disderi (1819-1890) who had a studio on the Boulevard des Italiens in Paris. At that time the price of a studio portrait of 10 in by 8 in was 50 to 100 francs (£2 to £4) and he realised that this was too much for the average person. He patented a process of taking ten photographs on one glass plate. The advantage apart from the reduction in the initial cost was that as the actual image was small, the customer could not insist on retouching.

In 1854 Disderi applied for a patent for *carte de visite* photographs. In May 1859, sixteen months after Orsini had failed to assassinate him, Napoleon III was leading his army off to Italy when he stopped outside Disderi's studio and went in to have his portrait taken. The resulting

Very early use of photography for an identity document, 1886.
In this French Portrait d'Identité the holder's likeness has been attested
by the photographer and his assistant and his signature witnessed by
the town hall. Another three decades were to pass before photographs
became commonplace on identity documents

publicity can be imagined. Disderi became the Court photographer and, as a result, immensely rich, at one time said to be taking £48,000 p.a. in his Paris studio. He spent as he earned but the boom did not last for ever. Although he diversified, he finished his life as an impoverished beach photographer in Nice.

In England, *carte de visite* photographs did not gain popularity until a photographer published an album of photographs of the royal family. Suddenly the images of their beloved queen and her family were available to the common people. The cards were small enough to be carried without damage and inexpensive compared to a studio portrait. Mayall, the originator of the craze in England, charged a guinea (£1.05) for a dozen cards and by the 1870s retail cards of famous people sold for 1s or 1s 6d. (5–7$\frac{1}{2}$ p).

It was the invention of the roll film which really liberated photography. The 'film' was a paper treated with a base coating which took the place of the glass negative. By 1885, George Eastman in the USA had established a company to make roll-film holders to fit on the backs of cameras and to take his celluloid-based roll film. In 1888 the first Kodak went on sale. It took 2$\frac{1}{2}$-in circular pictures, 100 of them, and the camera weighed 1$\frac{1}{2}$ lbs. It was enormously successful because of its ease of use and moderate price.

In the early years the factors of cost and practicality discouraged a serious consideration of using photography for passports. The cost of the copper or pewter plate would have far outstripped the fee for the passport and a foolproof manner of fixing it to a document would have been extremely difficult to devise. Nevertheless, the possibility of using a photograph as an aid to establishing identity had occurred to some. In 1851, the idea was raised fruitlessly by Dodero, a Marseille photographer and in 1853 a Monsieur V. Verneuil, described as 'a literary character', proposed to the French Minister of Police that a likeness of the holder should be taken by the daguerrotype process and placed beside the holder's signature on the passport. He had even found an artist who would undertake to do it at a cheap rate and a chemist who would make it indelible.[4] No further details were given and although the Minister assured him that the suggestion would be taken into serious consideration, nothing came of it.

A decade later in England, the humorous publication *Punch* suggested:

> ...that photographs be used henceforth as passports. Every traveller should have his *carte de visite* taken and attested as his likeness before he starts from home: and the production of this portrait should be an open sesame at any frontier gate. Pen and ink descriptions are usually so vague that they scarcely ever serve to identify a person: and what is said about one's 'age' or one's 'visage' in a passport is not merely not flattering but often strangely incorrect. A photograph of course would give a far more faithful picture and one that might at any rate more easily be recognisable than any written catalogue of one's features, age and height...[5]

Advanced though these ideas were, they were out of phase with the mores of the time since by the 1860s many European countries were thinking more about abolishing passports altogether than of how to make them more complicated. For a passport to carry a photograph, two things were needed: a cheap, durable photograph which could be easily and permanently attached to a passport, and a reason for needing it. The former was eventually supplied by the invention of the roll film and the latter by spies such as Lody.

The worldwide response to the First World War was that suddenly countries demanded that a photograph be fixed to a passport. The US Department of State was unable to

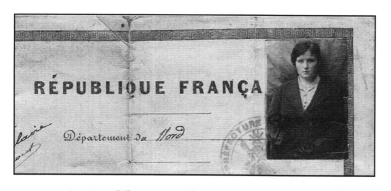

Where to put the photograph?
When the French passport form was designed in the 1880s
it was not provided with a space for the photograph which
would be needed by the time this passport was issued in 1920.
The title should read: REPUBLIQUE FRANÇAISE

produce immediately a passport designed to bear a photograph and so, to fill the gap before a new design was ready, the old passports were used and the issuing officer was required to attach the photograph to whichever part of the sheet he could find unencumbered by endorsements. It was not until 1917 that the USA began using a format which had a space for affixing a photograph. The same problem presented itself to all the countries – the documents were just not designed to carry a photograph. The result was that sheet passports were issued where the photograph partially obscured the name of the country or the personal description of the holder and in the booklet-form passports the photograph was pasted on the first available empty page and this could be some way into an already partially filled passport.

In 1915, the UK introduced a new passport design which incorporated a photograph and was a spectacular improvement on its predecessor. It boasted, at last, a proper description of the bearer, a fixed term of validity and space for renewals, a printed set of regulations and an area designed to receive visas. Although it was protected by board covers bound in blue cloth and bearing a gold blocked crest, it was still a single sheet of paper, in this case now pink, which was folded so as to fit within the covers. Holders of passports in the old format of white folded sheet which had hardly changed for eighty years, were required to have their photographs affixed to the front, usually the top left corner, which was the only free space available.

The early poses used in passport photographs were the artistic ones of the Victorian photographer, sometimes complete with the imitation waterfall or plywood balustrade so beloved of the nineteenth century cabinet photographer. If you wore a hat, then you were photographed in a hat.

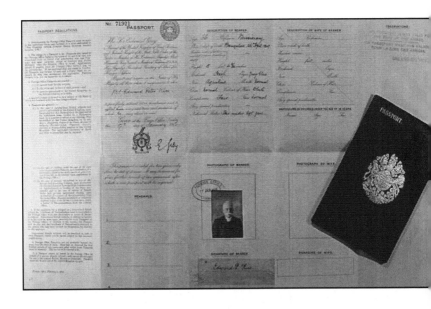

The first British passport to be designed to accept a photograph was introduced on 1 February 1915. Although, like the version which it replaced, it was still a single sheet of paper, it now folded into a blue card cover and for the first time gave a full physical description of the holder.

This 1915 British passport photograph demonstrates that the formal 'passport pose' had not yet developed.

Photographs had been used socially for many decades and the idea that a passport photograph should be different in any way did not occur at first to the authorities. The regulations for the passport photograph on an application form for a British passport in 1920 were contained in a sparse footnote: 'Duplicate small unmounted photographs of the applicant (and wife if to be included) must be sent, one of which must be certified on the back by the recommender.'[6] It was not until later that the following refinement was added: '...These photographs should be printed on thin paper and measure not more than 3 inches by 2 inches or less than 2$\frac{1}{2}$ inches by 1$\frac{1}{2}$ inches. They should be taken full face without a hat.'[7] Specifying thin paper for passport photographs was necessary since the *carte de visite* photographs which they so resembled were traditionally mounted on a stiff card backing which made them quite unsuitable for attachment to a passport. Some authorities indicated the kind of clothes which should be worn for the photograph; the USA suggested that street or travel attire was appropriate and that hats should not be worn unless they were part of a religious attire worn daily.[8]

The question of how to attach the photograph to the document was important since, if the photograph could be detached and replaced by another, then it would be that much easier for the spy or criminal to pass frontiers fraudulently. Now that documents bore photographs it was human nature to check the photograph and ignore the written description unless some suspicion had already been aroused and thus a skilfully replaced photograph could easily carry a credible imposter through.

The simple staple was very quickly shown to be fallible. It could easily be unbent and re-formed. Applying an ink or embossed stamp, part on the photograph and part on or through the page, made swapping photos more difficult. Some countries used special rivets, extra strong glue, signature slips or intricate wafers pasted over one edge of the photograph; some even added thumbprints. In the 1930s the photograph was fixed into a US passport by the expedient of pressing it with a laundry type flat iron to bond the bookbinder's paste to the photograph.

The teething troubles were soon mastered but although it was obvious that the photograph met the identification requirements of a passport to an extent and detail hitherto

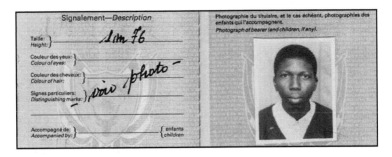

Expecting too much of a photograph?
In this 1990 Niger passport the section 'colour of eyes
colour of hair' has been endorsed *'voir photo'* – see photo.
The photograph is black and white.

unknown, the authorities seemed loath to fully trust it. Thus an officer issuing a passport of the Kingdom of Belgium in 1920, after pasting into position the photograph of the bearer, still had to fill in a list detailing hair, eyebrows, eyes, forehead, nose, mouth, chin, face, beard and height.

Twenty years later, some countries were still duplicating the work to this extent, however, reliance upon the photograph can be taken too far as the ilustration opposite shows.

Now that the photograph had been adopted, little else was required of it. As the passports became booklets in the early 1920s so it was found that the dimensions of the image needed to be reduced to fit within the covers and because the stiffness of a photograph covering a large proportion of a page would make the booklet difficult to handle.

The popular demand for photography encouraged many improvements in the equipment available to the public. While the local photographer evolved into the local photographic shop, the demystifying of photography led to a decrease in his studio work. No longer was it an occasion to have one's photograph taken. The *carte de visite* boom was well and truly over but, despite this, the natural vanity of man still brought him to the studio for his passport photograph and many passports of this time bear witness to the studio quality of their photographs.

There were periods, however, when the mere acquisition of a photograph became difficult. In France during the German occupation of 1940–45, photographic materials were strictly rationed and controlled and yet identity cards and residence and travel permissions proliferated. The resourceful French satisfied the demand by repairing to their family albums and selecting snapshots to be attached to their cards. Thus one can find identity cards bearing, for example, a photograph of the holder taken at the seaside or even one where the holder's image has been cut from the middle of a group photograph.

War shortages forced the holder of this 1943 French identity card to use a photograph from her family album

Britain's wartime response to the increase in demand for identity photographs was to form a committee. The Camera and Accessories Sub Committee of the British Standards Institution was convened on 9 October 1940 to draw up a War Emergency British Standard for Identity Camera Picture Sizes. This was considered to be urgently required by government departments. Quite magnanimously, they invited a representative from the Passport Office to attend these meetings since they recognised that the result of their deliberations might impinge upon the work of that department. Events were to suggest that it might have been sensible to have also invited a representative from the photographic industry.

Just before Christmas 1940, the Sub Committee produced its draft standard which dealt with the size of identity pictures, the types of sensitised materials to be used with identity cameras and even the minimum focal length of the lens permitted. The detail was painstaking. The photographs were to be either 2in by 2in or 35 mm by 23 mm. For the 2-in size photograph they decreed that the film should be $3^{1}/_{4}$ by $2^{1}/_{4}$ 8-exposure roll film numbered to give 12 exposures and suggested that suitable films would be the Barnet, Gevaert and Selo Spool no. 20, the Ensign spool no. E20 and the Kodak spool no. 120.

The recommended focal length of the lens was to be $5^{1}/_{2}$ in with a minimum permissible length of 4 in and the pose of the picture should be such that the distance from the top of the head to the chin consisted approximately one half of the overall height of the photograph.

The draft standard was a model of bureaucratic punctiliousness, unfortunately it had one great fault. At what must have been an embarrassing meeting on 11 February 1941 they had had to consider the observations of Mr J. Mitchell, an employee of the photographic company Ilford Ltd. He had pointed out that the camera that they had specified, did not exist – there was no such camera in Britain. The ordinary lens for the roll-film camera was 3 in which was an inch less than their permitted minimum and few owners of 35 mm cameras would have possessed lenses of focal length 4 in or longer.

The reason that the Committee had laid down minimum focal lengths was to ensure that the image size would be great enough to permit contact printing whilst avoiding the effects of the distorted perspective which results when a camera is moved close to the subject.

Mr Mitchell suggested that any camera would do as long as it produced a good print of the correct size, even the glass plate cameras used by the Victorian *carte de visite* photographers should not be ruled out. Indeed, he could not understand why the type of camera needed to be specified at all. The Committee apparently agreed, for their final standard was simply that photographs had to be 2 in by 2 in for a head-and-shoulders portrait full face and without a hat to be printed on thin paper.[9]

The increasing need for photographs for identity purposes did not pass unnoticed by the industry. This was something that they could understand. It was a standard, uniform product needed hundreds of times per day and in which there was only one variable factor: the customer's face. It cried out for automation. The instant developing process which had been first commercialised in the Land cameras manufactured in the USA in the 1940s was adapted to meet this need. The first automatic photo booth was opened in 1946 and by the 1960s they were a common sight. It is so convenient nowadays to use such a facility that it is difficult to imagine what life was like without it. No appointment is necessary; all that is required is that you put the correct coins in the slot and set the stool to the appropriate height.

Continuing technical progress has brought in colour photographs which were first used in US passports in February 1958, and photographs processed digitally and printed directly onto the passport page, which were first used in Japanese passports in November 1992. Although these developments represent progress and are without doubt, innovative, are they actually improvements? The photo booth negative is smaller and thus records less detail than that of the photographic studio it usurped and the lighting is not individually set by a photographer according to the tint of each face. One might expect colour photographs to be more representative but the quality of the colour can be doubtful and the tonal contrast effect of black and white is reduced. The digital photograph cannot be removed from the page and can easily be transmitted from the computer data bank to anywhere in the world, but the pixelation – the breaking up of the photograph into dots – reduces its definition and accuracy.

Photograph in a
Czechoslovakian
passport of 1931.

The quality of
studio passport
images of the early
twentieth century
puts present-day
photographs
to shame

It seems that in this search for technical progress the purpose of a passport photograph – to look like its bearer – has been lost. And yet one might wonder if ever it did look like its bearer. The old adage that when you begin to look like your passport photograph then you know that it is time to return home is perhaps not so wide of the mark and an observation such as that from Miss Frances G. Knight, the director of the US Passport Office in 1957, that people looked thuglike and abnormal when sitting for their passport photographs, is hardly likely to endear them to the image which is then produced.[10]   From its early days travellers have entertained a love/hate relationship with their passport photograph.   They resent its unforgiving record but have to recognise its passe-partout usefulness. This is epitomised by the observations of an American wife in the 1920s who, whilst admitting that her passport had enabled her to enter Japan with her two children to join her husband, nevertheless could not resist the temptation to ridicule that constituent part of her passport which had been so persuasive in its function:

> ... a likeness of myself taken in a studio reeking with blue lights which specialised in passport pictures delivered in an hour, adorned my passport. That photograph would have convinced anyone that I was a poignantly mournful-visaged mulatto but it bore across it the official stamp of the United States asserting it to be a picture of me and the Japanese Immigration Authority tacitly insulted me by accepting it as a faithful likeness....[11]

6

PERFECTION ITSELF

During the latter half of the nineteenth century, the Passport System in many countries had either fallen into disuse or been discarded. Norway abolished its system in 1859, Sweden in 1860, Italy in 1861 and Portugal in 1863. After the fuss which had been caused by Orsini in 1858, France quietly abandoned its passport system two years later, relying upon residence permit regulations for foreigners staying for longer than three months although it did reintroduce a passport requirement for the duration of the Franco Prussian War of 1870–71. Across the Atlantic, many South American countries such as Venezuela, Uruguay, Mexico, Ecuador, Bolivia and Peru enjoyed constitutions in which the right to freely travel without a passport was clearly stated and extended to all foreigners. However, British male travellers aged between seventeen and forty five, visiting Uruguay during the civil unrest of 1896 discovered that a passport could be vital to prevent them from being picked up in the street and forcibly enrolled in the National Guard.[1]

The United States introduced a passport requirement for a short time during the Civil War in 1861 but by the end of the century Alvey A. Dee of the Department of State in Washington was proudly proclaiming that there was '....neither law nor regulation in the United States requiring those who resort to its territories to produce passports.[2] The requirement for Chinese to have identity papers in order to disembark was not a passport imposition, of course, it was a private agreement made between the governments of the USA and China to enable certain classes of Chinese to enter.

In some countries the irrelevance of the passport was made quite apparent. The Persian foreign minister, in explaining that printed regulations regarding passports did not exist in Persia, observed that, 'Aliens entering Persian territory are supposed to show their passports on the frontier but the rule is seldom enforced on a European traveller of respectable appearance,'[3] The rules of the Sultanate of Muscat were a little more forthright: '[there are]...no regulations for foreigners or passports in the Sultanate of Muskat and no sort of impediment is imposed by local authorities against foreigners wishing to travel to the interior, however it is unsafe to do so without an armed escort of adequate strength.'[4] Greece admitted that there existed an old law of 28 March 1835 which still required passports but that it had fallen into disuse. A similar situation obtained in Martinique with a law of 1850, also disregarded. In Switzerland the law in each Canton was different but a foreigner staying for longer than a holiday could avoid any requirement for a passport by staying at a hotel and not in lodgings.

By the beginning of the twentieth century, passports were in most cases a facility or a politeness, they were not a requirement. Only Bulgaria, Roumania, Russia and Turkey obliged every foreigner to obtain a passport, properly viséd before arrival and demanded a passport from all of its nationals wishing to leave. Some countries used the system to control their own population either for its own good or the good of the country. Italy would not issue exit permits to its subjects wishing to emigrate unless they held travel tickets. Germany required passports from any of its male subjects wishing to leave who were liable for military service and although Hungary had a passport system, nobody took any notice of it and no checks were made.

The suggestion in many of the contemporary guide books that passports were not needed for travel but were essential for reclaiming packages at the post office, gaining entry to museums and changing money might seem flippant today. The truth was that foreign post offices exercised a stricter control over whom they released poste restante items to than their governments exercised over whom they allowed to enter the country and many banking houses would not accept a traveller's foreign money for exchange into local currency unless he presented a letter of introduction from his own bank or was introduced to them by a local worthy known to them.

Given this situation, it was quite natural that the risingly vociferous anti-passport lobby should entertain every hope that all countries would see sense and that these odious documents would soon become extinct. The First World War cruelly dashed these hopes. Suddenly spies were seen to be everywhere and national security was considered more important than international facility. All controls were intensified and rather than a decrease in the number of documents, new documents were invented.

The reality of war allowed governments to introduce into law restrictive measures of a ferocity such as would never have been permitted in peace-time whilst cynically qualifying them with the assurance that they would be lifted once peace came. The citizens of the United Kingdom, for example, with the passing of the National Registration Act in 1915 which obliged them to carry identity cards, found themselves subject to the kind of internal control that they had so ridiculed and despised on the Continent.

The USA discovered that with the increase in the number of Government officials travelling to Europe it needed to extend its passport umbrella. They felt that whilst this growing body of persons did not enjoy diplomatic status they should nevertheless be differentiated

The British Government used the outbreak of the First World War as a reason for introducing a system of national registration of the population. For many generations the British had despised and ridiculed such systems operating on the Continent.

from the *hoi-polloi*, if only to render their circulation in suspicion-minded Europe a little less onerous. Thus they gave the world the 'special passport' in 1918. Used by high ranking servicemen, non-diplomatic members of legations and their families and officials on government business, the passport's existence obliged other countries to invent a 'special visa' so that they could endorse it.

At the end of the war in 1918, the movement to abolish passports re-energised itself but it was now fighting governments who had discovered how closely a population could be controlled and how easily this could be justified. And the regulation was not necessarily aimed only at former belligerent nations. In maintaining the visa requirement for passengers coming from North America after the war, the British Government was ready to parry any protest from the USA. '...it is possible therefore that a protest against the maintenance of the visa system may be made by the US govt. but the recent labour unrest in Canada seems to prove that the US cannot be disregarded as a centre of Bolshevik propaganda...'[5]

It was clear to all parties no matter what their belief, that in the restless turmoil of post-war Europe, with the hordes of humanity crossing borders daily, a concerted approach was needed. The route for this was provided by the League of Nations in Geneva with its Provisional Committee on Communications and Transit. This called together an International Conference on Passports, Customs Formalities and Through Tickets in 1920. It was to be 'charged with the study of the methods necessary to facilitate the international passenger traffic by rail at present more especially hindered by passport and customs formalities as well as by the difficulties of obtaining through tickets...'[6] The committee recognised that these factors were: '...a serious obstacle to the resumption of normal intercourse and to the economic recovery of the world.'[7]

One of the most far-reaching proposals was that in order to expedite control during a journey the signatory countries should agree on a uniform style of passport issued to identical standards and to supersede all present passport issues. This resolution, which was passed by the Conference in October 1920, invited the governments to adopt the measures with as little delay as possible and they fixed the date for introduction of the new passport at 1 July 1921 – eight months to design, print, bind, distribute and issue a completely new passport.

The physical characteristics of the 'international passport', as it was named, were that it should contain thirty-two pages, all numbered. It should be in at least two languages – the national language and French. Its size should be 15^1/$_2$ cm by 10^1/$_2$ cm. It should be bound in cardboard, the front cover bearing on the top the name and in the centre the coat of arms of the country and the bottom the word 'passport'. Also, it should only be issued for a single journey or a period of two years. The validity of the passport issued for two years could be extended. The fee charged should not be of a fiscal character and would be collected without any discrimination between countries for which the passport was issued and with absolute equality as between 'nationals' and 'non-nationals' in the event of a passport being issued by a government to persons other that its 'nationals'.

The response to the 'international passport' from the signatory countries was quite revealing of the economic and political situation of the time. Many countries adopted the passport proposals without demur – Australia, Austria, Canada, Czecho-Slovakia, Greece, India, Luxembourg, New Zealand, Romania, South Africa, Siam, Spain and the United Kingdom. Some had minor observations or reservations to voice – Belgium liked the wording but had it printed onto its current single-sheet passport. Bulgaria baulked at the idea of not earning a revenue and declared that: 'The Royal Government of Bulgaria in view of the extremely precarious financial situation of Bulgaria cannot consent to a regulation that the fee charged shall not be of a fiscal nature.'[8]

The Chinese government declared its willingness to establish a uniform type for ordinary passports but explained that in view of the vast extent of the Chinese Republic and the very numerous bodies entitled to issue passports it would require a considerable time to give effect to this measure. The Danes were very enthusiastic and

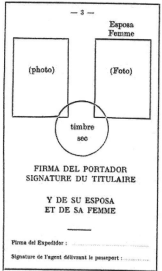

The exact size of this passport should be : 15 ½ × 10 ½ cm.

In 1920, the League of Nations Conference on Passports, Customs Formalities and Through Tickets proposed this design for a standard international passport.

printed their document in four languages instead of the recommended two. Finland, perhaps feeling the closeness of Bolshevik Russia, was unwilling to accept the idea of a visa being valid for the entire life of the passport. It felt that hostile states might take advantage of visas thus given for an indefinite period to send their propaganda agents into the country. Hungary adopted the 'we will if you will' attitude with a rider that this particularly applied to the states bordering Hungary. Sweden was worried that insisting upon a uniform type of ordinary passport would encourage forgery and fraudulent reproductions.

Norway agreed with its neighbour and pointed out that whilst they accepted the idea of a uniform passport, the proposal should not extend to a diktat on the type, quality or colour of paper, inks and watermarks used, since these were the very idiosyncrasies that would help to identify individual countries' documents and make the work of the forger that much more difficult.

Japan's rather ingenuous plea highlights just how novel pan-global negotiating was at that time:

> In principle the Imperial Government sees no objection to the establishment of a uniform type of ordinary passport but it ventures to point out that the difference of character and custom in Europe and America are likely to prove an obstacle to the desired uniformity as far as Japan is concerned. The fixing of July 1st. next as the date for the issue of new passports clearly affords Japan insufficient time to make the necessary changes in procedure and to print and prepare the new forms.[9]

European conceit had prevented delegates from realising how uncomfortably some of their customs would sit with other cultures. The booklet passport layout as suggested by the Conference was fine as long as everybody started at the 'front' of the book and wrote from left to right.

The sobering notice from the Italian Government in a 1924 passport.

'Warning to Emigrants

'Citizens are advised that to be protected and supported by
the Emigration Law, if they wish to go to America they must take
an emigrant steamer with tickets issued in Italy from authorised
agents. Emigrants must refuse all proposals from foreign
emigration agencies offering embarkation in foreign ports,
acceptance of which might incur serious disadvantages;
greater expense, longer journey, lack of protection on the
ship from government officials, requirement to resort to a
foreign court of law in case of dispute and the expense of
waiting embarkation in a foreign seaport.'

All these countries were, however, in favour of the
concept and positive in their response to it. What of the
dissenters? Italy was quite candid. It declared that the
passport was the only effective means at its disposal for
regulating emigration and preventing immigration into
countries where it was impossible to procure work. This
was Italy's response to unscrupulous employment and

emigration agents. South American countries were crying out for labour and the agents promised all sorts of rewards in order to entice workers abroad and then renegued on their promises, leaving the immigrants with the choice between slave labour and starvation. Italy decided it would keep its current passports which were drawn up in Italian only and in which they would affix a photograph if other countries required it.

The Netherlands declared categorically that the proposed passport was 'not practicable' without explaining why and stated its intention to continue issuing its present passport. Its response to a series of resolutions under the same Conference concerned with the standardisation of visas was a bit more revealing. It rejected them on the basis that because of the housing and unemployment crisis, the Netherlands had been obliged to reduce rather than extend the period that a visitor could stay in their country and they needed to retain that option of curtailment.

Poland agreed with the idea but was unable to fix a date for its introduction because it desired to retain its present passport which was valid for one year only, to enable it to continue its policy of identifying and defining its own nationals. This was an important consideration for a country which, as a result of the peace settlement of the Treaty of Versailles, had acquired more territory, in this case from Upper Silesia, and with it, additional population.

But the most clearly argued and thorough rejection of the proposals came from France. On cost alone it would not consider the new design. Its present single-sheet passport cost 102 French Francs per 1,000 to produce. They had costed out the new 'international passport' at 441 French Francs per 1,000 which would need them to quadruple the price of their passports. This they declared was unacceptable to the government especially – as they insisted – there were grounds for believing that 'the passport system would shortly be abolished.[10]

Similarly the French would not agree to the extension of the validity of the passport beyond two years since, in their opinion, a passport after two years would be so worn that it would require replacement. One could observe with impartiality that the single-sheet passport that they were retaining would almost certainly wear less well in two years' use than would the proposed card-covered booklet. Finally, they added their own recommendation to the effect that the French Government was quite prepared to join in agreements for the abolition of passport formalities. It had already done so with Belgium and Luxembourg and had approached Great Britain with the same suggestion.

The overall aim of the Conference had been to facilitate international rail travel by making improvements in the areas of tickets, customs formalities and passports. From the geographical standpoint of the United Kingdom, the initial results were a little alarming. Of the three countries through which Britons were most likely to transit, France and the Netherlands had rejected the passport proposals outright and Belgium had adopted the wording but not the format.

These obstacles aside, the resolutions of the Conference were to have an indelible effect for decades to come upon the passport design of many countries, the United Kingdom in particular. In interpreting the recommendations, in 1921 the UK gave birth to the famous and durable dark blue passport booklet which was to remain in production with various modifications for another seventy years. This passport resembled the foldout passport of 1915 which it replaced, in that its pages were pink and the cover was dark blue with a gold-blocked crest. The card of the cover, however, was now sturdier to better support the two cutouts in which the passport number and the holder's name were entered so as to be readable from the front cover. The tightly bound close-stitched spine was designed to ensure longevity and resistance to fraud which could otherwise be perpetrated by the removal and replacement of pages in a stapled or simple-stitched booklet.

When the Conference convened again in Geneva in May 1926 to assess the progress made towards the 'international passport' and agree and propose improvements, the British passport was upheld as 'perfection itself'.[11] It was recommended for adoption to those countries who had not yet produced an 'international passport'. This suggestion was not received favourably by all. Estonia and Poland, for example, in rejecting the technique of entering the name

The United Kingdom's first booklet passport, seen left, was introduced in 1921 and followed closely the suggested design of the League of Nations' Conference of 1920.

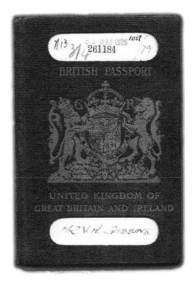

When the Conference reconvened in 1926, it described the latest version of the UK passport, seen right, as being 'perfection itself'.

of the holder and the passport number on the cover declared that there could be little advantage in doing this since they would be very soon effaced and they observed that the method of inscription employed by Great Britain for this purpose would be very costly.[12]

The intention of the Conference was not to try to get the British 'perfection itself' passport model adopted by all but to promote the universal design of which the British interpretation appeared to be the most desirable. The Conference's success, although only partial, was in absolute terms, quite astonishing. It had managed by 1929 to change utterly the face of passports worldwide; replacing designs that had been in use with no real modification for sixty or seventy years and this in less than a decade. The Conference's influence even extended outside the membership of the League of Nations. In 1926 the United States, not a member of the League, introduced its type III passport which was roughly the $10^{1}/_{2}$ by $15^{1}/_{2}$ cm size laid down by the Conference and it had a stiff dark red cover with a window cutout to view the number and a total of 32 pages. Its internal layout differed slightly from that of the 'international passport' but the influence was obvious.

Whilst one side of the League was pondering over passports, tickets and Customs procedures, another section was facing a far more serious problem. At the end of the First World War the populations of the world were all mixed up in Europe but it was not a simple matter of sending them home. Once the combatants had returned surplus soldiers to their homelands, the plight of the prisoners of war had to be settled. By the end of 1919, the majority of German and Austrian prisoners who had been held in allied camps were back in their own countries but the hapless soldiers who had been taken prisoner by the Russians were still detained in Siberia, trapped by the inertia which followed the Russian Revolution of 1917. There they remained, weakened by cholera and famine, dying in their hundreds.

Approaches by Western countries to expedite their release and repatriation were met by Russian intransigence and suspicion. The latter's response was understandable when one considers that several of those Western countries were in the process of trying to overthrow the Russian government even whilst they negotiated. As late as 1919, thousands of British troops who had been garrisoned at Archangel were pledging their support to the Russian Admiral Koltchak who had set out to march on Moscow in an attempt to overthrow the Communist rule.

The League of Nations looked for a credible person to negotiate with the Russians – somebody who would be respected for impartiality and seen as a humanitarian rather than a partisan. Their choice alighted on the Norwegian polar explorer, Frijdthof Nansen and they appointed him High Commissioner with the special responsibility for repatriating these prisoners. Nansen, with immense application and organisation and much negotiation and coercion, had managed by 1922 to arrange the transport home of 430,000 prisoners of more than twenty different nationalities.

Having solved that problem Nansen was then presented with a more difficult task and one which was becoming more acute every day – the problem of the refugees. Added to the civilians who had fled the fighting in Europe during the First World War were $1^1/_2$ million Russians who had sought sanctuary from the troubles in their country; troubles which could only have been exacerbated by the Western countries trying to topple their government. Refugees do not stay to fight, they vote with their feet and cross the nearest border. Thus the Russian refugees fled into Turkey and Poland, into the Baltic states of Latvia, Lithuania and Estonia; some, like the remnants of Koltchak's reactionary force, fled eastwards into Korea, Japan and China. An outbreak of cholera and typhoid followed hard by famine squeezed the Russian peasants from their land. Contemporary estimates showed 600,000 refugeees in Poland, a half a million in Germany, 70,000 in the Far East and 150,000 in Turkey. Romania received 30,000 Jews who had fled persecution in the Ukraine. Turkey also had turned upon its minorities and expelled the Kurds and the Armenians. Europe became an ant heap pullulating with unwanted people.

The efforts of the charities, the government-sponsored aid organisations and the donations from benevolent foundations were all channelled towards relieving the immediate poverty and hardship. Shelter, food and health were the urgent requirements of the refugees and all the available aid was not sufficient to provide it. Nansen could see that it would never be sufficient; a different approach was needed. Armed with an analysis of the refugees' employment skills obtained from a census undertaken by the International Labour Organisation, he set about trying to find a home and employment for them all. Nansen strongly believed that there was room for them all, if not in Europe then somewhere in the world and they had no need to starve, for work was available. The main belligerents in the war had lost millions of young men, their work force had died in the trenches. France, for example, was a country of old men, women and children and was in dire need of miners and agricultural workers.

Nansen soon pared the problem down to one of documentation. No matter how badly a country wanted workers, it would not admit people without passports because that meant that eventually they would not be able to get rid of them – no other country would take them. The reason why most of the refugees had no valid documents was that Russia had cancelled the passports of any Russian living outside Russia and refused to revalidate passports unless the holders returned within its frontiers. It needed a working population as much as any other country and it believed that the best way to obtain one was for its own workers to return home. Naturally, this was not a view shared by the refugees who in many cases had fled to save their lives.

Nansen found a key to the deadlock. If no country would accept these people and issue them with passports then the League of Nations would do so. He invented a document to be issued valid for a period of one year to enable a refugee to cross frontiers and remain in a country and work. With a proportion of his wages the refugee purchased stamps from the League of Nations in order to pay the fee for renewing his passport for a further year. The revenue provided by these stamps actually financed another round of passport issues which in turn generated more revenue. By 1924, France had taken in 400,000 Russians as workers. Many found new homes in the South American republics and by the time that Nansen died in 1929, the refugee problem was largely under control.

This was an extraordinary solution. The authority which issued the passports had no country, it had no territory, it had no population – it was supranational – but thanks to its perceived status, the holders found work and a security of sorts. The League of Nations passport was known as the Nansen Passport and it carried that title printed on its white paper cover. It must be the only example in the world of a person giving their name to a passport.

The Peace Settlement at Versailles created 8,000 kilometres of new frontiers in Europe. Empires were broken up and new countries created and these needed passports. They had no cause to resort to the kind of resourcefulness that Benjamin Franklin had shown a century earlier in copying a French passport, for, thanks to the International Conference on Passports, they were presented with a finished product – the 'international passport'. Four of the new countries: Finland, Estonia, Latvia and Czecho-Slovakia found themselves able to adopt the passport immediately.

A Nansen passport issued in Bulgaria just before the outbreak of the Second World War.

НАНСЕНОВЪ ПАСПОРТЪ

УДОСТОВЪРЕНИЕ ЗА САМОЛИЧНОСТЬ

ВАЖИ ЗА ЕДНА ГОДИНА

24 СТРАНИЦИ   СТОЙНОСТЬ 5 ЛЕВА

№ 01688

PASSEPORT NANSEN

CERTIFICAT D'IDENTITÉ

VALABLE POUR UN AN

24 PAGES   PRIX 5 LEVAS

Elsewhere in Europe the territorial situation impressed a diverse influence upon identity documentation. The area of Germany which lay between the west bank of the river Rhine and the eastern frontier of France was declared a demilitarised zone and was occupied initially by allied troops to maintain its demilitarised status. In order to travel to this area – known as the Occupied Rhineland – no matter what passport a person held, a special safe conduct was required.

Not all the divisions of territory and population were achieved in a single act. Some areas were designated 'Plebiscite Areas', such as the Saar or Klagenfurt. Here the populations were governed by an impartial caretaker administration on the understanding that within a certain time a plebiscite would be held to determine which country a safe conduct permitting a French lady to visit the 'Rhineland occupied by the allied armies' in 1926.

the people belonged to. In order to prevent an interested country from trying to influence the results in its favour by exporting additional members of its own population to the Plebiscite Area, passports had to be endorsed on the territorial restrictions page, 'Not valid for travel to Plebiscite Areas'.

The Second World War was followed by a period of austerity, suspicion and recrimination rather as the First World War had been. Europe was carved up once again and across its ruins tramped millions of 'displaced persons' but this time no help could be expected from the League of Nations and its Nansen Passports since both had ceased to function at the outbreak of the war in 1939. In an attempt to move the non-Germans out, the Military Government of Germany issued a document entitled 'Temporary Travel Document in Lieu of Passport for Stateless Persons and Persons of Undetermined Nationality'. Once this had been endorsed with the visa of the receiving country, then the displaced person could leave Germany. Nothing was needed for the Germans within Germany – they were going nowhere. They could still be issued with the German identity card, the *Kennkarte*, by their local town hall.

Initially, because of the shortages caused by the war, the officials had to use the stock of documents and rubber stamps that they possessed and these were emblazoned with an emblem which was now a ghastly embarrassment – the swastika. Thus the *Kennkartes* issued immediately after the cessation of hostilities in 1945 had a German eagle pasted on the front cover to hide the swastika and the circular rubber stamps endorsed inside bore the name of the issuing town around their rim but sported a blank centre where the swastika had been cut out.

A shortage of materials in Germany after the Second World War forced the authorities to use the Nazi stamps after cutting out the swastika in the middle.

1942   **1945**.

 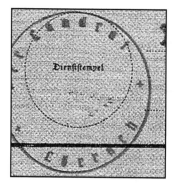

Little by little the various post-war currency and travel restrictions were lifted and the public were allowed to venture abroad again. The British 'perfection itself' passport remained in favour at home and with and many of the Commonwealth countries, although as the status of some of the latter began to change in the 1960s, it seemed that their first desire after leaving the Commonwealth or becoming independent within it, was to reject a design that may have reminded them too much of British colonialism.

Countries outside the British Commonwealth also began to drop the design for many varied reasons. One important influence must have been the increase in air travel and the change in fashion. The British blue passport was designed in an era when most international travel was achieved by train and much intercontinental travel, by ship. Passports were carried by men – the majority of women who travelled did so by accompanying their husbands and were entered on his passport. With the expansion of air travel came a change in habits. The passport controls were increasingly conducted before the traveller had been reunited with his luggage. This meant that the passports had to be carried in hand baggage or on the person. It was not convenient to carry a large-format inflexible booklet in the lighter and less cumbrous clothing that the general improvement in travelling conditions now permitted. Many countries switched to a smaller booklet with a flexible cover. It was easier to issue and to endorse because it would lie flat, unlike the hardback stiff-bound version and as a bonus it was cheaper to manufacture and lighter to transport.

But the final nail in the coffin of the 'perfection itself' passport was the fruition of a desire which had been burgeoning for decades, tantalisingly unattainable until man discovered an application for one of the most common elements to be found on earth – silicon.

7

PROBABLY WE'LL LIVE TO
SEE MACHINES DO IT

The first application of machines to the issuing of passports was centuries old and fundamental – printing. The change from the handwritten document to the pre-printed form onto which a clerk made manuscript entries was a natural progression which brought several benefits.

One, the saving in time, was little important to the issuer of the passport during the era when, compared to modern times, few passports were issued and those that were, went to moneyed or influential personages. The individual then charged with the task of issuing the passport was probably more concerned with the saving in physical effort from not having to write out a page of flowing script. However, as the popularity of travel increased, it became more and more important to be able to reduce the amount of time taken to produce each document if only to be able to avoid accumulating a backlog. However, the service could be of a rapidity unrecognisable today. In the nineteenth century, for example, the British Foreign Office stated that, 'Passports are issued at the Foreign Office, between the hours of 11 and 4, on the day following that on which the application has been received at the Foreign Office...'[1]

This kind of celerity fostered in travellers the habit of applying for passports at the very last minute, sometimes only two or three days before their ship was due to sail. They would be unaware of the total number of applications received daily at the Foreign Office. When the demand increased, doubling and tripling the workload of the same number of clerks, the applicants still expected to receive their passports within a couple of days of asking for them and still made their travel arrangements with that assumption in mind. The move to a pad of pre-printed passport forms, torn off individually as required and then completed in ink allowed the authorities to meet this demand with a success that would have been impossible had the same human resources been applied to writing out the entire text of each passport in longhand.

With the saving in time came a saving in money, not only from greater productivity with the same size workforce, but also from the economies of scale. The batch printing of passports on machine-manufactured paper reduced the unit cost to a level against which an ink-dipped plume scratching across handmade paper could never compete.

Printing also allowed greater uniformity and security. Once the functioning text of the passport had been established it was correct on every issue – there would be no spelling mistakes or lapses of grammar from a clerk or consul working under pressure. To combat counterfeiting, once one highly skilled craftsman had engraved an intricate and impressive design on a steel plate, it could then be used to print the emblem faultlessly on every passport for years to come. The result could be a document of uniform clarity, crisply printed on banknote style paper which would act as an ambassador of the issuing country every time it crossed a border.

Having introduced the printed pro-forma which required only a few handwritten entries for its completion, it was inevitable that man should wish to continue to the natural conclusion: a printed form with printed entries. For this, a mechanical writing machine was needed.

116

A passport that permitted Don Francisco de Mata, an infantry officer, to travel from Madrid to Barcelona in 1836.

Listed overleaf is his entitlement to rations of bread and wine from the towns on his route.

Commercial typewriting machines began to appear on the market in the USA and Europe in the latter quarter of the nineteenth century. Initially seen as a novelty, they were noisy and cumbersome and in the early days, actually slower than writing by hand. They were clearly unsuitable for issuing passports. Ironically, by the time that sufficient technological improvement had been made to allow them to be considered as candidates for passport use, the latter had become a booklet which could not be fed into a typewriter.

Some countries persevered and the Canadian passport of the 1930s, for example, was completed on a specially adapted typewriter made by a company called Elliott-Fisher. Not wishing to be left behind by a member of the Commonwealth, the British Passport Office investigated the practicability of using this system for British passports but had to reject it for several reasons. One disadvantage was that £2,000 would be needed to purchase the twenty Elliott-Fisher machines necessary to achieve the peak daily total of 2,000 passport issues. It was felt that this would never be recouped from savings in staff time. Also, the 'perfection itself' passport required entries on three pages and the time taken to insert and withdraw the booklet three times would reduce the time saving to between 10 and 20 per cent. Finally, and probably the most damning; the stiff, secure binding of the passport would prevent the machine from making a decent impression on the paper at all. [2]

The problem of how to roll a passport around a typewriter platen without breaking the spine would not be solved for another twenty-five years. Although, in 1928 the USA had brought in a hard-covered passport to resemble the League of Nations Conference proposals, the Type V, introduced in 1932, had reverted to soft covers. This enabled the Department of State to use a flatbed printing machine to enter the holder's details. It was a far from ideal system, being slow and tiring for the operator who had to depress a foot pedal to release and insert a passport but it did produce a uniform result in a specially designed typeface of upper case letters only, composed of dots.

In 1956 the US Department of State made the breakthrough with a specially adapted electric typewriter working to an ingeniously simple idea. Instead of rolling the passport vertically around the platen – a procedure guaranteed to damage the binding – the passport was inserted horizontally and the spine was slotted into a groove on the platen which protected it from being crushed.

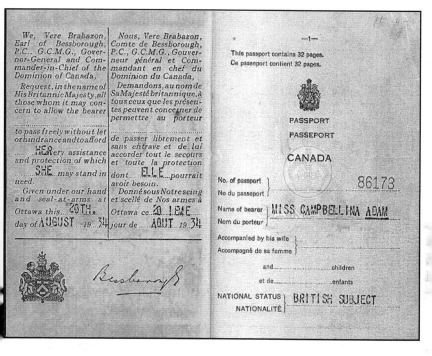

The inflexibility of a booklet-style passport, bound in hard covers presents serious difficulties when entries are made using a typewriter. The unevenness of the typed text in this Canadian passport of 1934 bears witnesss to this.

The passport was also reduced from thirty-two pages to twenty which created less bulk in the machine. By turning the format of the page through 90 degrees, a format known as 'landscape' as opposed to 'portrait', it was possible to type in the entries quickly and clearly on a modified but commercially available electric typewriter.

It seemed that once machines had got their foot in the door there was no stopping them. Two years later the USA introduced a further refinement in adapting the punched tape processor from teletype machines to operate its electric typewriters. As other countries brought in their own systems of typewriting, more and more passports appeared in the horizontal format. The effects of this trend when added to the 'back to front' format of some Oriental and Arabic passports gave passport-control officers worldwide the invigorating challenge of trying to recall whether to open the passport at the front or the back and whether it needed to be twisted sideways in order to be read and if so, which way.

There were planners who were even thinking about replacing the passport-control officers with machines. Equipment to read text was already in use in the banking system, reading thousands of cheques per day by scanning the specially designed numbers printed thereon. Why not use a similar system on passports? As with the introduction of photographs, two stimuli were needed: the desire and the capability.

The desire came not from a particular government or foreign ministry but, rather as in the case of the League of Nations, from an international body. In this case it was one heavily interested in the swift passage of people through border controls: the International Civil Aviation Organisation which was founded in 1946 as an agency of the United Nations Organisation. Foreseeing problems in handling the increase in the numbers of passengers that was predicted once the Jumbo jet became operational, the ICAO began to investigate solutions. It was at this time that the results of the commercialisation of the silicon chip circuit began to exert a widespread and deep influence on the way analysts thought about systems. Electronic computers which had previously filled a room were now ten times more powerful and could sit on a desk. Shortly they would be portable and cheaper and yet even more powerful. Some predicted that one day they would read passports and recognise faces.

The ICAO began its meetings in 1968 with the aim of the member countries agreeing an international standard for the layout and specification of a passport. In the climate of technological innovation then prevailing, it was inevitable that they should consider how to make a machine-readable passport, known as an MRP. This would be a document which would be inserted in a machine of some design which, having scanned the passport and read the name and details of the holder, would perform a function necessary to facilitate his passage through the control point. Perhaps the ultimate aim was a frontier control rather like that on a rapid-transit system with passengers processing their own passports to open a gate.

Unlike the League of Nations Conference, the ICAO did not agree on a design and get it introduced in the space of eight months: it took ten years to agree the specifications. The ICAO's solution was to reduce the passport to the basic functions of establishing nationality and identity and these, they propounded, could be fulfilled by the use of a plastic card rather like a bank or credit card, charged with the necessary data in a form to make it machine-readable.

One of the important decisions was to specify that all the details to be scanned by the machine were also to be easily readable by the human eye. This was not only a failsafe in case of machine breakdown, it was a matter of civil rights. The principle of encoding information on a magnetic strip was already being used successfully on hundreds of millions of bank and credit cards across the world but they could not be read by the naked eye. None of us actually knows what our bank card says about us when it is passed through a reader. The ICAO decided that there were to be no secret or discreet marks or codes to be used for whatever purpose; every passport holder should be able to read all the information about him that was contained on the document. For this reason the technology used was Optical Character Recognition (OCR) which gives a machine the ability to read a script that a human can also read.

Interestingly, the idea of a card-type passport was not new; it had been suggested by the infant ICAO itself twenty years earlier at the United Nations Conference on Passports and Frontier Formalities which was held in Geneva from 1947 onwards. The Consolidated Statement of Proposals issued at the start of the 1947 conference contained amongst other ideas, a motion to return to the pre-1914 regime wherein passports were not compulsory and the suggestion of the ICAO that passports should be simplified by the adoption of a card-type passport. This document was to be called a 'Tourist Card' and would only be available to non-immigrant travellers. It would contain descriptive details of the holder, a photograph and a statement of nationality and would be recognised by all the subscribing countries.

In 1947, the USA dismissed it as being 'not practicable' but the Belgians had already been making it work for over a quarter of a century – the national identity card to be used as a passport. This 1919 card allowed the holder to travel freely through Belgum, the Netherlands and Luxembourg.

The American delegate Mr Tait responded vigorously to these proposals by observing that: 'The universal abolition of the passport as a compulsory entrance requirement is not desirable at present, but bilateral or multilateral agreements to waive it should be explored...'[3] He further recommended that the League of Nations type passport or an improved version 'such as the US passport'[4] should be used with a minimum validity of two years, which, coincidentally, was the validity of the US passport of the time. As for the suggestion of a 'Tourist Card' type passport, he dismissed this as 'not practicable'[5].

The British delegation, led by Mr C. Carew Robinson, Assistant Under Secretary of State at the Home Office, also proposed standardisation around the League of Nations type passport but with a five-year validity, renewable for five years and costing the equivalent of 15*s*. This, as it happened, was exactly the same as the British passport then being issued.

Belgium, which had been slow to adopt the League of Nations passport in 1920, now in 1947 took up the cudgels against the American delegate's dismissal of the card-type passport. Belgium's Mr Schneider pointed out that not only was it practicable, but it was being used currently and had been used by Belgium for some time. Their identity card was exactly that. It had to be held by every Belgian over fifteen years of age, it carried a photograph and had the same guarantees as a passport. The cards were issued by the authorities of the commune in which the holder lived and all details of birth, nationality of parents etc. were verified.[6] That a small, European state, impoverished by six years of debilitating warfare could produce and use a document which the most powerful nation on earth had declared impracticable, must have caused as much embarrassment in some quarters as it had glee in others.

The Second World War had only been over for two years. The physical scars were ever-present and the psychological ones had an undeniable influence on the thinking of the delegates. In the resumé of the passport regulations currently applied in the individual countries, the Polish delegate, Mr Przezwanski, considered it quite natural that Poland should allow German nationals to only travel westwards in their country. In the discussion on collective passports, Mr Perier, the French representative remarked that naturally, none of the concessions France agreed to would apply to the nationals of enemy states. When the USA declared that the whole concept of collective passports was contrary to its policy, Mr Schneider declared that Belgium had been issuing them for some time and that they were cheaper and made the frontier control quicker. Considering the cost of issue of a document in terms of the amount of paper it required was apparently one which did not come into the cognisance of the American delegates, living as they did, in a country of plenty. During the debate on how best to inform the traveller of customs tariffs, Mr J. Van der Poel of the Netherlands remarked rather tartly that it was all very well for the USA to suggest issuing a leaflet to each traveller but the Netherlands could not see how they were to procure the paper on which to print it.[7]

The Conference sat through long flowery speeches by Mr Nan-ju Wu, on how open his country, China, was to visitors and it nodded through points of procedure put by Mr Przezwanski. The meeting concluded that passports could not be abandoned but the way forward in this area was to abolish visas reciprocally. It was probably the visa requirements of various countries which suggested to the USA that the tourist card-type passport would not work, for there would be nowhere on it to stamp a visa. Belgian nationals were able to use their identity cards as passports only in countries with which Belgium had concluded visa-free agreements.

The Conference delegates agreed to maintain the *status quo* with regard to passport design, i.e.: the 1920 League of

Nations layout as amended in 1926 was the best product. The French delegate, Mr Perier, insisted on the deletion of the reference to an 'improved version such as the US passport' although the conference did make it clear that any improvements to the design should be used.[8] And so the card-type passport slipped back into obscurity until the ICAO and the advent of the silicon chip awoke it, but before it was to be put into use in Europe, another big shake-up was necessary.

On 5 May 1949 the foreign ministers of ten European states met in Strasbourg and signed the statute of the Council of Europe the aim of which was to achieve a greater unity amongst those states for the benefit of improved social and economic progress. The Council did not waste much time for in August of the same year the Consultative Assembly discussed nationality laws with the ultimate object of creating a common European nationality and a European passport. On 8 September they approved the following recommendation: 'Recognising the importance of the question of a European passport both in itself and by reason of its importance as a gesture, the assembly recommends to the Committee of ministers that each member state should ensure that the question of a European passport should be studied by its appropriate departments of state.'[9]

In Britain the proposal found little favour. It was difficult to define what was to be the relationship between the proposed European passport and the existing national passport. If the European passport was to give a greater accessibility how was this to be achieved without imposing restraints on the national passports which already worked perfectly? The problem was that a common nationality was still a long way off yet without it, the universal European passport would have no reason to exist. It could only be an equivalent of a national passport and whilst the Committee recognised the importance of the European passport as a gesture, producing another style of passport to run concurrently with those existing whilst conferring no extra rights upon its holder would certainly be seen as an empty and rather ridiculous act.

'Member State of the Council of Europe' printed in French and Flemish at the top of this Belgian passport was the nearest approach any country made to a European passport in 1964.

The fact that a common passport could only function if a common nationality existed was one which Britain knew from its own affairs for it had just presided over the dissolution of the first uniform passport that the world had ever known. Its 'perfection itself' passport had been used by citizens of many of the member countries of the British Commonwealth for travel throughout the world. The design had only required minor amendments for each country – perhaps the wording on the inside front cover designating in whose authority it had been issued or the impression of the country's name on the front of the cover. Wherever one travelled in the world, a passport of a British Commonwealth country was instantly recognisable. It actually fulfilled the desiderata of the Council of Europe but for the member states of the British Commonwealth. With the coming into law of the British Nationality Act of 1948, Commonwealth countries had been obliged to define their own nationality. Some members decided to underline this change with a move away from the British passport design; many followed suit in later years.

The proposals of the Council of Europe with regard to a common document for travelling had little effect although Belgium with its customary enthusiasm in these matters, did then issue passports endorsed with the epithet, 'Member State of the Council of Europe'. Another twenty-five years were to pass before the question of a universal European passport was to be raised again and this by the Passport Union Sub Committee of the European Economic Community, as it was then known.

One of the avowed aims of the EEC had always been the abolition of frontier controls within the Community; the control was to be effected at the point where the person first entered the Community from a non-Community country. Once inside, the person should then be free to roam at will. It saw the corollary to this as being the creation of a uniform passport to be issued by all the member countries of the EEC. The first meeting was held in 1974 and whilst the Euro-pundits were arguing over details such as the colour of the cover, lilac being favourite at one point, the ICAO was already getting to grips with the revolution that the silicon chip had effected. Six years later, the politicians had to admit, rather shamefacedly, that an important proportion of their discussions had been rendered obsolete by the advance of technology. It would seem that civil aviation interests considering their profit margin were more productive than politicians dithering over ideologies.

When the European Parliament finally passed its resolution in Strasbourg in 1980, it decided that the European Passport was to be machine-readable...eventually.

Britain supported the incorporation of the plastic machine-readable data card as suggested by the ICAO. It pointed out that the card would need to be part of the passport and not the entire passport since a booklet would still be needed for the endorsement of visas and frontier stamps for countries outside the EEC.

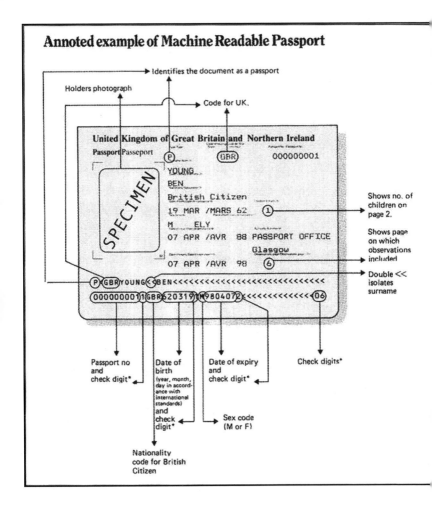

How to read the first UK edition machine-readable passport.

Indeed, outside the EEC, progress was quicker. The USA was first to introduce an MRP in 1981 followed smartly by Canada and Australia and by 1983 the USA had issued about four million MRPs. The advantage gained by the traveller in the early days was minimal. The MRP was simply an interesting curiosity for the other countries since they did not possess the machines to read the passport and would have no intention of installing any until they were almost ready to issue their own MRPs. The UK's first experimental machine-readable passport desk was installed at London's airport, Heathrow and came into service in April 1983.

The long-awaited marriage of the needs of the civil aviation industry to the ideological aspirations of the European Unionists finally gave birth to the European model MRP. Britain issued its first European MRPs in August 1987 and began to phase out its dark-blue passport in 1990. The dark-red cover of its replacement, bearing the additional title 'European Community' above the royal coat of arms, was as a red rag to a bull for a vociferous group of Britons who complained long and loud about losing the 'right to be British' and resented the suggestion that they were in any way European. Some fanatics travelled abroad to renew their passports at British consulates which in the early days were unable to issue the MRP and were still using a stock of blue passports. Such are the ironies of immigration rules that the UK was issuing a version of the red MRP which did not mention the European Community anywhere upon it. It was reserved for a select tranche of its subjects who although British, had no right to live in the UK. Some British passport holders found the change quite unsettling for in renewing a dark-blue, hard-covered passport which opened and read like a conventional book they had been given given a small red booklet which opened at the back like an Arabic passport, but had to be read sideways.

The horizontal format for the MRP was inescapable. The details needed to be entered in the passport by a typing machine in the special font which had been designed for easy reading both by machine and human. Also, in passing through the frontier control point the two lines of data needed to be inserted in a slot in the reading machine and this required them to be at the edge of an unobstructed cover or page.

The Passport Union committee of the EC had seen its aim as doing away with the 'passports of varying appearance currently issued' in order to replace them with documents 'which would symbolize a definite connection with the Communities[10]. This they hoped would assist them to negotiate visa agreements with non-EC countries whose benefits would be common to all EC members. The premise was that once the foreign country had agreed a visa or entry requirement for all members of the EC it would only have to refer to the distinctive passport to confirm in its mind the entitlement of the holder to that agreement.

The first editions of the EC uniform passports which were issued failed utterly to convey an aura of uniformity. Granted, the covers all bore the legend 'European Community' but the colours of those covers varied from deep burgundy for the Spanish passport to a pinkish magenta for the Dutch document. An inspection of the interior was more damning. The French version was standard book format and handwritten with a clear plastic laminate covering all details except the signature. The UK version opened at the back, as did the Spanish, with all the machine-readable data and photograph on the inside back cover, completely covered by clear laminate. The Danish had a soft plastic cover and the horizontal format necessary for machine readability but was handwritten and not an MRP, whereas the Portuguese was standard book format and machine printed but not machine-readable. The Dutch was practically the same book-format passport as the

1950 model it replaced and in which colour photos were still not permitted. Coupled with the adoption by non-EC countries, such as Thailand, Colombia and Dominica, of similar formats and colours, the distinctiveness of the EC uniform passport failed to make its mark.

Subsequent versions of the passports have moved nearer towards uniformity. Interestingly, the only country to adopt from the outset the plastic data card idea suggested by the ICAO and then promoted by the UK, was Germany whose national identity card is identical with the data page of its passport. In order to protect the card from damage and prevent it from ripping the pages of the booklet, it had to be contained between stiff card covers; the only EC passport that was.

In the search for more and more accurate ways of describing an individual – establishing the 'bio-data' as it is called – a system has now been invented where a passenger first submits to a computer scan of his eyes. The passenger is then issued with a plastic card upon which the bio-data relating to his irises have been recorded digitally. When he arrives at an airport provided with the appropriate facilities, he introduces the card into a reader, looks into a camera as he walks through and if he has the right eyes, he is allowed to pass.

The Dutch set up such a system at Schiphol Airport, Amsterdam in January 2002; a month later a similar trial was started at Heathrow Airport. As with the introduction of the first MRPs, the system can only be an interesting curiosity until all ports and all passengers are appropriately equipped.

It is arguable whether frontier controls have speeded up as a result of the introduction of the MRP, and the degree of influence that the latter might have exerted on border checks is impossible to calculate. The introduction of the MRP was accompanied in many cases by a simultaneous revision of the overall control procedure. Whether the member countries adopted the MRP for its ability to speed up controls remains a point for discussion. The passport-control officers are still there. It is they who operate the passport-reading system not the passenger. Running the passport through the machine does not result in a gate automatically swinging open but an instruction appearing on the screen in front of the officer, telling him what to do with the passenger. Once the document has been read, the data can be sent to any computer on the system – to the police, the intelligence service, the tax authorities – and in a nanosecond or two an objection to, or an observation about the holder can appear on the screen. Whereas before, the officer could only look up selected passengers on the 'black list' because of the time implications, now everybody can be checked, even nationals of one's own country who might not actually need to be controlled for passport purposes. Similarly, the number of names on a black list would have been dictated by the size of book that could be physically handled at a control point; with a computer it is practically limitless.

Is it too cynical to wonder whether it was the possibility provided by the silicon chip to vet every passenger in the twinkling of an eye, to know where they physically were in an instant, that persuaded governments to adopt the MRP? It seems that with the introduction of the machine-readable passport, George Orwell's *1984* was dead on time.

8

PASSPORTS CAN SERIOUSLY DAMAGE YOUR HEALTH

The land around Flensburg on the border of Germany and Denmark, lying as it does on a peninsula between the Baltic Sea and the North Sea, can be a cold, damp and draughty place in May and in 1945 this was no exception. It was early in the evening of 28 May and two British army officers, Captain Lickorish and Lieutenant Perry, were walking amongst the trees, collecting wood to make a fire. They had noticed a man watching them in their task and now his apparent aimless wandering seemed to bring him closer to them. Although the German armed forces had unconditionally surrendered more than two weeks earlier they were aware that there could still be some dangerous individuals roaming the countryside, unwilling to disarm, hoping for at least one last crack at the enemy.

The two British officers eyed the man warily but he looked more like a harmless refugee than a fanatical fighter. He presented the typical profile of the thin and undernourished civilian, dirty and unkempt, his clothes shabby. They continued to collect wood. He continued to watch. Suddenly he called across to them, '*Il y a encore des morceaux ici,*' indicating some broken branches. They moved towards him; he seemed to be making an attempt at affability and his French was not that of a German. 'There are a few more pieces here,' he repeated in English. At the sound of his voice intoning their native language, the two soldiers looked sharply at each other and then drew off to confer. Lieutenant Perry was certain of his hunch. He had heard that voice before. He returned to the man. 'You wouldn't happen to be William Joyce would you?' he asked.

The man put his hand in his pocket but before he could draw a weapon, Lieutenant Perry unholstered his revolver and shot him in the leg. He fell to the ground protesting that he was Fritz Hansen. It had been his German passport in that name that he had been trying to pull from his pocket, for he was unarmed. Unfortunately for him, when they searched his other pocket they found a German military passport in the name of William Joyce. The most despised traitor of the century, the German radio propaganda broadcaster reviled in England as 'Lord Haw Haw', had been captured.

That Joyce was a traitor nobody doubted. He held a British passport, he had gone to Berlin at the outbreak of the war and had broadcast anti-British propaganda from Germany for five years. He had 'adhered to the King's enemies' in the quaint terminology of the Treason Act of 1351. But the antiquity of the laws of treason threatened to provide some difficult and unwanted complications to the trial.

A charge of treason would have to be heard under the Treason Act of 1800 which included certain unrepealed sections of the 1708 Act and the 1695 Act. These sections, which were now held to be obsolete, laid down the procedures to be followed and they reflected the relative unreliability of the judicial processes in the seventeenth century. For example, one section required that at least ten days before the trial, the prisoner be given a list of the witnesses and of the jury. This was intended to prevent 'packing' a jury. In order to facilitate the running of the treason trials which would inevitably be called after the Second World War, the Government proposed a new law, the Treason Act 1945. This would repeal some of the ancient and outmoded sections of the older acts and was intended to simplify procedure sufficiently to make the running of a treason trial largely similar to a murder trial. Joyce was kept in hospital in France until the act had been passed and then he was brought to England the day after so that his trial would be the first to benefit. One part of the 1695 act which was repealed by the new act was the requirement for there to be at least two witnesses both to the same overt act or one to each act of overt treason.

As it turned out, the prosecution produced only one witness, to only one act – Police Inspector Hunt. He had been stationed at Folkestone at the outbreak of the war and was familiar with William Joyce's voice from having heard him speak at meetings. He testified that while listening to the radio in Folkestone on 10 December 1939, he recognised the voice as Joyce's when the announcer said, 'Folkestone and Dover have been destroyed'. This was the only witness called to the overt act of treason. It is not certain that a second witness would have been available since a successful witness would have had to have been able to recognise Joyce's voice and to have heard him broadcast. A charge of treason could only stick if the offence had been committed whilst Joyce's British passport was valid. The passport had expired on 2 July 1940 and most of his early broadcasts consisted of simply reading the news. It was only later that his 'Jairmany calling, Jairmany calling,' became so well known and by then, Joyce was a German citizen.

And then there was the question of Joyce's British passport. How had he come by it? William Joyce was born on 24 April 1906 at 1377 Herkimer Street, Brooklyn, New York. His father, Michael Francis Joyce had been British, born in 1869 at Ballinrobe, Mayo, Ireland. However, before William was born, his parents had gone to the USA and his father had been naturalised there on 25 October 1894, renouncing his British nationality in order to do so.

William, therefore, was unequivocally American – native born of an American father. How could a British court charge an American with treason?

The family had left the USA and returned to Ireland in 1909 and lived in Mayo and Galway. In 1921, Joyce, at the age of fifteen, came to England. His family followed a year later. He first read science at the Battersea Polytechnic but then graduated from Birkbeck College in History and English. Whilst studying, he applied to join the University of London Officers' Training Corps, stating that he was born in the USA of British parents and that his father had never been naturalised. This claim was not denied by his father who stated in support of his son's application that the family was British. This was untrue. Michael Joyce was still an American and his son, Willliam, had never been anything else.

William Joyce's political awareness began to manifest itself and by 1923 he had joined the British Fascists whose main occupation at that time seemed to be to fight with the Communists. In 1928 he did a year's post-graduate course in philology followed by a two-year course in psychology at King's College, London. During his spare time he assisted and spoke publicly for the Conservative Party. In 1933 he joined Sir Oswald Moseley's British Union of Fascists and the following year he appeared in court in Worthing alongside Moseley and was acquitted of the charge of riotous assembly. In March 1937 he formed his own political party, the National Socialist League which had an office in Park Street, Bristol.

By 1939, his political activities had brought him to the attention of the authorities and it is almost certain that a 'gating circular' was issued to immigration officers at all ports to prevent him from leaving the UK. On 24 August 1939 he renewed his British passport for a further year. This passport had been issued to him in 1933. On the application form he had claimed to be British by birth and

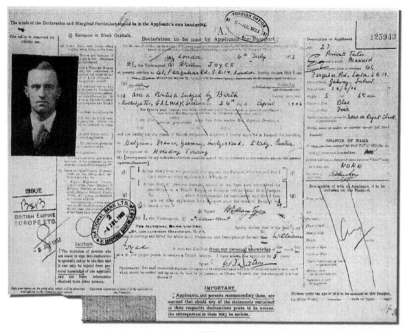

The lies that killed William Joyce.

Above, Form 'A', completed in his own hand in 1933 and on which he applied for a British passport by claiming to have been born in Galway, Ireland. Right, Form 'D' – the final renewal of that passport which he made on 24 August 1939 in order to travel to Germany. On it he has clearly written, 'British Subject by Birth'.

Applicants are warned on Form 'A' that should any of their statements prove to be untrue, 'the consequences to them may be serious.'

to have been born at Rutledge Terrace, Galway, Ireland. This lie had been given credibility by the endorsement of his bank manager who had believed it to be true. On 27 August 1939 he dissolved the National Socialist League and shortly after this he successfully evaded the watch at the ports and left the UK.

Acquiring a British passport by fraud does not make one British. Joyce was still an American. In September 1940 he took German nationality. Had he been British he could have been charged with this misdemeanour for it was an offence to take up the nationality of a country of the King's enemy but Joyce was American and in 1940, America was not at war with Germany. When he was captured he was trying to proffer a German passport in a false identity but he had retained his German military passbook which proved his true identity and German nationality. So this was the man that the British judicial system had charged with treason.

At his trial Joyce did not dispute the facts of his broadcasts from Germany; upon capture he had made a lucid statement detailing his actions and explaining his reasons. The thorny problem remained that the court was trying for treason a man who was not, and had never been, British. Very little assistance on this subject could be drawn from the Treason Acts themselves for they did not mention the concept of *nationality*. Mr Justice Tucker therefore opined that the question of *allegiance* was paramount. Joyce had lived as if he had been British, had renewed his fraudulently obtained British passport and had thus enjoyed the protection of the British and so he owed allegiance to the British Crown. In broadcasting from Germany he had betrayed that allegiance and thus had committed treason. Before a learned declaration such as that the jury could do nothing other that find Joyce guilty which they did and he was sentenced to death on 19 September 1945.

Joyce appealed on the grounds that the court had no authority to try an alien for an offence against British law committed in a foreign country. He stated that as an American and then a German he had at no time owed allegiance to the British Crown and there was no evidence that the renewal of his British passport had afforded him any protection provided by the Crown. The appeal was dismissed on 7 November 1945. He appealed further, to the House of Lords, on 10 December 1945 and this was dismissed eight days later. On 3 January 1946, Joyce was hanged at Wandsworth Prison; killed by a British passport he should never have had.

A prisoner under sentence of death is allowed certain privileges and to comfort Joyce in the last few days of his life, his wife, Margaret, was brought over from her prison camp in Germany. In an ironic twist of inhumane logic, the authorities returned her to Germany after his execution for, under the nationality laws, although originally British, as a married woman she acquired the nationality of her husband and this, as they recognised by returning her to Germany, was German.[1] Joyce discovered with an appalling finality that a passport was not just a harmless little book with a photograph inside that you waved about when you went on holiday; it purported to give you rights and demanded duties in exchange.

A modern passport performs two main functions: it establishes the identity and the nationality of its holder. In Joyce's case both were irrelevant since he admitted his identity and the authorities ignored his nationality. It was the concept of allegiance that was invoked to condemn him, but allegiance is not referred to in passports, they only mention citizenship and nationality. The passage of time has somehow fused and confused the ideas of allegiance, nationality and citizenship. This is a potentially dangerous situation given that one of these, as we have seen, can kill you.

The concept of allegiance in history is ancient. It was understood, accepted and expected, both by the monarch and his subjects. There was no need to define or delineate it. You had a king, you owed allegiance to him. It was as simple as that.

In Roman times the rules of citizenship were clearly laid out in law. In essence, there were two levels: the common level attributable to all persons living in the Empire – Latin Citizenship, and the upper level – Roman Citizenship. Your status dictated to whom you paid your taxes. A Roman citizen paid them directly to Rome, a Latin citizen paid them to the local administration. It was generally more beneficial from a financial point of view to be a Roman citizen and to hold any positions of responsibility, it was essential.

As an alien in the Roman Empire, you could acquire either citizenship by various acts and achievements. For example, an enemy alien who defected to the Roman side during a battle, bringing with him information that enabled the Roman army to secure victory, could be given full Roman citizenship. As an ordinary civilian, after a certain number of years service in the Roman civil service, one might be rewarded with citizenship.

With the rights came duties, one of which was military service. Refusal to submit yourself for military service would result in your citizenship being taken away. One might have hoped that the possession of the citizenship of the most powerful empire then in existence might serve as reassurance and protection, as no doubt it did in most circumstances, however, in one area it abandoned you utterly just when you might need it most. Romans automatically lost their citizenship on being made a prisoner of war.[2]

By the thirteenth century in England, the concept of allegiance was beginning to be mentioned in a legal sense in statutes of the realm. By the middle of the fourteenth century, the question of a person's entitlement to inherit when born outside the realm to English parents, hinged around whether or not the parents owed allegiance to the king.

Thus far, there was no mention of nationality for the truth is that 'nationality' as a word was not in common use until the early nineteenth century whereas 'allegiance' has its roots in Middle English or earlier. The English probably drew their word 'nationality' from the French *principe des nationalités*. This was a revolutionary theory which said that

Certificate of Citizenship issued by the Supreme Court of New York in 1935 to a British national on his being naturalised as a citizen of the USA

persons having a common language and culture form a nation and as such, ought to be entitled to self-government as a state. The idea was certainly given a fillip by the declaration of the *Convention*, the new French Legislative Assembly formed in 1792, that it was ready to assist all oppressed peoples to overthrow their rulers. It can be appreciated that in the sprawling pan-racial empires of nineteenth-century Europe, such as the Austro-Hungarian Empire and the Ottoman Empire, the suggestion that national groups should be self-governing generated as much fervour in the hearts of the peoples themselves as it did fear in the minds of those ruling them.

By 1850, the word 'nationality' had its equivalent in most of the European countries; even more numerous were the definitions of it. This situation had not been in any way clarified by the actions of the revolutionary governments. For them, the words 'allegiance' and 'subject' were far too redolent of monarchy and so both the USA and France, upon changing their status, adopted the word 'citizen' or 'national' to describe what would have formerly been called the 'subjects' of their country.

Several South American countries such as Nicaragua, Colombia, and Ecuador, issue passports which do not state the nationality of the holder. The presumption is that the passport is only issued to nationals of that country.

But the prize for creating confusion in establishing the nationality of its subjects must go to Britain. At the beginning of the nineteenth century, a British passport did not as a matter of course state that the holder was a British citizen; it might make a reference to his being 'an English Gentleman'. By the end of the century the definition 'British Subject' had been adopted and the laudable situation obtained whereby this appellation was applied to the members of the British Empire worldwide, no matter which constituent country they originated in. This caused no problem while the Empire lasted but during the twentieth century, political developments made it necessary to change the description of national status in the UK passport for the British Empire evolved into the British Commonwealth, member countries became independent within and without it, and finally, the UK entered the European Union.

Thus, by the end of the twentieth century, the national status of British passport holders as described on their passports during that period could have been any one of the following:

British Subject,
British Born Subject
British Subject by birth.
British Subject by birth – wife of a British Subject
British Subject – Citizen of the United Kingdom and Colonies,
British Subject without citizenship
British Protected Person
British Overseas Citizen
British Citizen
British National (overseas)
British Dependent Territory Citizen
British Subject – the holder's status under the Immigration Act 1971 has not yet been defined.
Commonwealth Citizen

Some countries of the Commonwealth had more than one administration functioning within them. Nigeria, for example before gaining its independence within the Commonwealth, had the Colony of Lagos based around this important port and (then) capital city. The inhabitants of this area were designated 'British Subjects, Citizen of the United Kingdom and Colonies'.

The remainder of Nigeria was a protectorate and the inhabitants were thus classified as 'British Protected

Persons'. In the 1970s they defined their nationality in the following manner:

Nationality *Nationalité*
CITIZEN OF NIGERIA
A Citizen of Nigeria has a Status
of a COMMONWEALTH Citizen

Qualifying for citizenship under more than one heading was not unusual within the Commonwealth. Thus Jamaica described its citizens:

National Status *Nationalité*

Citizen of Jamaica and
Commonwealth Citizen

Fiji used the following until its independence in 1970:

National Status
Nationalité

FIJI CITIZEN AND BRITISH SUBJECT

Canada, although in the British Commonwealth, has a very important and active French minority and its passports reflect this.

The bearer of this pass-
port is a Canadian citizen.

Le titulaire de ce passe-
port est citoyen canadien.

Outside the Commonwealth, the politics of partitioned Europe perhaps suggested the ambivalent description used by the German Federal Republic in their passport. It avoided any mention of nationality or citizenship whatsoever but still conveyed with a characteristic succinctness what it meant.

> **Der Inhaber dieses Passes ist Deutscher**
> **The bearer of this passport is a German**
> **Le titulaire du présent passeport est ressortissant allemand**

The fundamental principles of the acquisition and loss of nationality differ little amongst countries which possess nationality or citizenship laws. The several routes by which nationality can be acquired are generally: by birth, descent, marriage, naturalisation, annexation or by some special consideration such as service in the Army. But it is rarely as simple as it sounds.

Nationality by 'birth' would seem straightforward until one considered foundlings, illegitimacy and adoption. In Madagascar for example, a foundling is presumed to be of Madagascan nationality unless counter evidence exists and in considering the evidence, notice is taken of the circumstances of the child's discovery and its physical appearance and manners.[3]

You do not always acquire the nationality of the country in which you are born if your parents should not have been there in the first place. Many countries refuse citizenship to children born of enemy aliens living in any occupied part of its territory and birth on a foreign-registered ship in international waters or on an airliner five miles up in the sky creates interesting complications.

In establishing your nationality by descent, the country may take into account both parents or just one and in considering marriage, your religious marriage may not be recognised by the country of your spouse and its duration may be of importance. In Malaysia, a woman acquiring Malaysian nationality by marriage, will lose it if the marriage is annulled in the first two years for any reason other than the death of the spouse.[4]

The acquisition of nationality by special consideration is sometimes promulgated in law. In Queen Anne's time it was considered that: 'Foreign mariners, having (during the war) served two years aboard British ships are to be deemed natural born subjects.'[5]

There have even been cases where nationality has been imposed on persons regardless of their current nationality. If you were resident in Brazil on 15 November 1889 and you did not lodge an objection before 14 May 1890, then you became Brazilian.[6] And nationality can be taken away against your wish. Some countries will withdraw their nationality from you should you engage in activities which it considers to be inconsistent with your being one of its nationals. Service in the armed forces of an enemy power is a fairly certain way of putting your nationality in jeopardy.

In Joyce's case, the possibility that his father might have had dual nationality, American and British, and thus been able to pass it on to William did not arise because the USA did not permit its nationals to hold any other nationality. In order to become American, Michael Joyce had been obliged first to renounce his British nationality in a Declaration of Intention with the words, 'It is my bona fide intention to renounce forever all allegiance and fidelity to any foreign prince, potentate, state or sovereignty, and particularly to Victoria, Queen of Great Britain and Ireland'.

Two very important exceptions to the 'nationality by birth' rule have been recognised for hundreds of years.

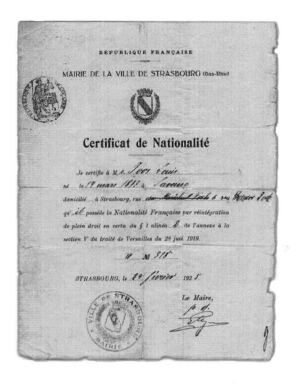

A Nationality Certificate issued in 1925, returning French citizenship to an inhabitant of Strasbourg after the settlement of the Treaty of Versailles. Germany annexed Alsace and Lorraine during the Franco-Prussian War of 1870-1. In 1919, France claimed back the territories and its population.

The child of a reigning monarch has the nationality of its own country, wheresoever it is born. The rationale for this is that it would be quite unacceptable if a foreign country could claim a member of another country's royal family as one of its own subjects. The other long standing exception, which was officially recognised and defined by a protocol in Vienna in 1963, is that applying to children of diplomats born in the country to which their parents are accredited.

They acquire the nationality of their parents, not that of the country of their birth. If the host country could demand allegiance of the diplomat's children, it would put him or her in a situation in which it would be impossible to carry out the diplomatic functions of representing his own country in the court of the other.

The question of Joyce's nationality had been debated, established and then discounted. His identity, after his first rather futile attempt at deception in the woods near Flensburg, had never been in question. Identity should be an easy attribute to establish. It is who you are and in everyday life is quite satisfactorily defined by your name. However, when you put your name into the context of the entire population then it loses some of its distinction. It is probably true that you are not the only person in the country or even in your town to use the name which you have come to consider as uniquely yours. To refine the definition of your identity, into your passport is added the date and place of your birth and sometimes your address. This usually suffices. The coincidence of another person existing with your name, place and date of birth is very unlikely and if one adds a parent's name to the definition of your identity then the mathematics of the probability of the existence of a duplicate approach the astronomical.

The paradox in this search for exact and unfailing identity is that in nearly every country which has a national system of taxation or social benefits, every member of the population is distinguishable from the cohort by a unique number.

The need for establishing a checkable identity is tied in with immigration control, which in turn is influenced by the state's attitude to migration of labour, state security and public order. When you present your passport to a passport-control officer he decides whether or not you are allowed into his country in accordance with the instructions and rules and laws of his country, not those of your country.

The diplomatic passport issued to the French Consul General taking up his post at Vera Cruz at the beginning of the Second World War

Checking somebody's name against a list may seem straightforward at first examination but naming customs differ throughout the world. In the Western Hemisphere we generally index persons under their family name but even within Europe, there are differences. The Spanish and Portuguese possess a double family name, but classify them differently. With the name Jose Gonzalez-Martins, for instance, if it were Spanish then Gonzalez would be the indexing name, if it were Portuguese, it would be Martins.

With some nationalities the surnames differ according to the sex of the holder. Thus in Polish Mr Latek would be married to Mrs Latkowa and although Russians have what we would recognise as surnames and they appear last in the line of names, it is generally the middle name which is most important. This is the patronymic name and is formed from the father's Christian name with the addition of the suffix *–vich* for a son and *ovna* for a daughter. Thus we know that Mariya Konstantinovna Borodin had a father whose Christian name was Konstantin.

A state without a nationality. A Vatican passport issued in the name of Pope Pius IX in 1858.

A traveller using a Vatican passport today is required by most countries to show also his national passport.

This verification is possible if you possess a family name but how does one identify people who do not have family names? The Arabs for example have one 'given' name. To this they can append as many of their father's given names as they wish, in reverse chronological order. So Mohammed whose father was also called Mohammed and whose father in turn was called Hussein would call himself Mohammed Mohammed Hussein although he could drop off the Hussein as and when he wished. It is apparent that this would have implications if you were searching for him in an index under the letter H.

Although Arabic uses a different script from the Roman and does not have the same concept of vowels as in the English language, a transposition into Roman alphabet is possible and fairly accurate. This is hardly the case for the most populous nation on earth which does not use an alphabet of letters but a catalogue of ideographs: the Chinese. An attempt to explain a Chinese name in Western terms albeit as simply as possible, is dauntingly complicated. To Romanise an ideograph into a form that a European can read and into a form of which he can approximate a pronunciation introduces a variant depending upon which Chinese language is being used, e.g. Mandarin, Cantonese etc. For example, the same ideograph could produce Chan, Tsan, Tan, Ting or Chen.

A standard Chinese name consists of three ideographs. The first is the Family Name, the second, the Generation Name and the third, the Personal Name. The Chinese readily claim that there are only about one hundred family names in use. Divide that into the population of China and you can see that establishing identity from a family name could easily call in some of the probability factors which we formerly dismissed as astronomical.

The Generation Name is a beautiful concept but one which only marginally refines the search. Each family, or clan, as defined by the family name, chooses or composes a poem to define the succeeding generations of the family. All the members of this generation then take the same ideograph from the poem as their generation name. So with the same family name and the same generation name for a group of people possibly all falling within an age span of twenty years, perhaps resorting to the personal name is the answer.

The personal name is almost an ephemeral concept in China. Upon birth, parents will choose a name for a child using whatever selection parameters they desire. As the child grows, in his early years the parents may then select an alternative personal name which they might consider more in tune with his physical or mental attributes. When the child later starts school, he may wish his friends to call him by another name and so will choose a new personal name. When he leaves school to start a job, involving as it does, moving into another circle of acquaintances, he may select another name and so on. All these names are officially recognised.[7] In cases as complex as these it is necessary to devise systems such as that used in Hong Kong passports where the name is codified numerically.

So the document that you carry in order to travel abroad is painstakingly effusive about your nationality and identity but is silent upon your allegiance and yet, like Joyce, you may not know that you have got your allegiance wrong until the noose is around your neck.

9

OUT OF THE ORDINARY

On 4 August 1914, Germany violated the neutrality of Belgium and Great Britain declared war on Germany. Sir Edward Grey, the British Ambassador in Berlin went to the German Foreign Ministry and called for his passports. The Russian ambassador had left Berlin two days earlier on 2 August and Cambon, the French Ambassador, left that afternoon. Grey returned to the British Embassy in the Wilhelmstrasse in front of which an angry crowd was already gathering. The mounted police were insufficient to prevent the crowd from throwing stones and smashing all the windows of the building. This latter act was a remarkable achievement for a supposedly unorchestrated gathering, given that all the surrounding streets were asphalted. Inside the embassy the staff were occupied emptying the safes and burning confidential documents.

On the following day, Sir Edward Grey met Mr Gerard, the American ambassador, and instructed him in the procedure to be followed for documenting British subjects trapped in Germany and then the seals were placed upon the embassy's archives. Whilst the embassy staff gathered the British press correspondents into the Embassy and organised a special train for their joint evacuation via the Netherlands, outside in the streets, British subjects were indiscriminately seized – men, women and children alike – and transported to Spandau to be imprisoned in the fortress there.[1]

A little before 6 a.m. on 6 August, before the populace of Berlin was awake, the Embassy officials made their way quietly to the railway station and boarded their train which would carry them westwards to safety. However, 250 miles away, a 22-year old British governess who had suddenly found herself to be an enemy alien, was frantically trying to get out of what was now a hostile Germany. She had no special train, she had no special passports – she was an ordinary person of the type that was being rounded up by the German authorities and shipped off to prison.

Despite being considered only an ordinary person, the lady was issued with an extraordinary passport for although she was a British Subject, the passport that enabled her to escape Germany was American. It was issued by the American Vice-Consul in Frankfurt under the instructions that he had received from his ambassador in Berlin, after the latter had concluded his meeting two days earlier with Sir Edward Grey. There is no doubt that this is an American passport – it is a single sheet of paper bearing the watermark of the American eagle and the large red Consular Seal of the USA is affixed at the bottom. The text at the top left corner, in explaining the reason for the issue of the document, must rate as a classic example of the meiosis of the time, 'This passport is issued... in view of the unusual conditions in Europe...'

A standard passport issued to a holder in conventional circumstances is termed an 'ordinary' passport but even ordinary passports have had idiosyncrasies which belied their description. The Cuban ordinary passport of the 1970s, for example, was only issued to persons who were leaving Cuba with no permission to return and the Honduran ordinary passport of the same period always stated it contained fifty pages but never contained more than forty-eight.

On occasions, a passport would suddenly become outdated by a change of government and the incoming

An American pasport issued to a British Subject to allow her to leave wartime Germany, 1914

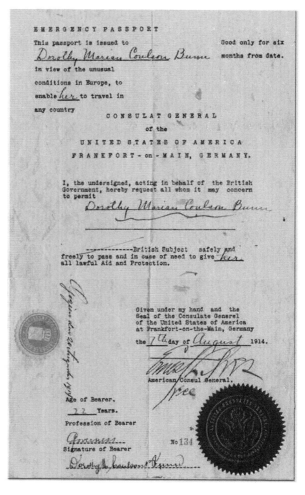

authority would not have the time to redesign a new emblem. In 1979, Iranian passports bore the title 'Empire of Iran' and so when the Iranian Islamic Republic was proclaimed in that year the documents were updated by a self-adhesive plastic label which was wrapped around the cover. During the constitutional revisions in Greece in the

1970s, the blue-covered Greek passport was modified by an unpreposessing square of black industrial tape which was used to obliterate the obsolete crest on the front cover.

Seen below is a British passport issued by the British Ambassador in Paris to enable a British Subject to travel to England in September 1871. On it, the ambassador has altered his title to reflect the change of government which took place during the Franco-Prussian War. The Foreign Office would not have had time to amend the passport printing plate and so the original text 'Empire of the French' has been overstamped with the words, 'French Republic', producing a rather messy result quite out of character with the rest of the document. It was this sort of slipshod modification which had caused the problem at Fiume recounted earlier.

A British passport issued in Paris in 1871. It has been officially modified to show the change in government from the 'Empire of the French' to the 'French Republic'.

Many countries issue several styles of passport according to their intended use. The most well known of the non-ordinary passports is the 'diplomatic'. This is issued to the country's ambassadors abroad and members of his family and the servants of his household. Often the umbrella of the diplomatic passport is extended to the consular officers and their families and servants. The function of this passport is to certify that the holder is covered by the various international conventions on diplomatic immunity. It was the possession of such documents that enabled the staff of the British Embassy in Berlin to leave Germany unmolested whilst the riff-raff with ordinary passports were rounded up and imprisoned. When Sir Edward Grey went to the German Foreign Office to 'call for his passports' this was a recognised procedure under international law. He already possessed a British passport – what he was requesting was his right to a guarantee that would allow him to leave the country with no hindrance. An ambassador 'calling for his passports' is the present day development of the ancient safe-conduct system.

The diplomatic passport usually differs outwardly from the ordinary passport in the colour of its cover. This enables the diplomat to be quickly passed down queues and it alerts the frontier control to the holder's immunity which also extends to his baggage. Sometimes, along with the title 'diplomatic passport', the colour of the cover is the only difference to distinguish the passport from the ordinary; in others, the text inside might state what position the holder enjoys or to which overseas post he is travelling. The UK used to be the only country which did not make a diplomatic passport – it stopped using such documents at the beginning of the twentieth century. Britain's diplomats were given the standard passport which carried a rubber stamp endorsement buried somewhere within its pages to the effect that, 'The bearer is a member of Her Britannic Majesty's Diplomatic Service.'

By Order of His Highness The Emir of State of Qatar, these special passports are issuable to members of the Ruling Family.

The issue of a special passport to any person other than a member of the Ruling Family is prohibited.

This special passport
was issued to members
of the Qatari ruling family
in the 1970s.

The hard covers are
gold-blocked and bound
in green leather

This bizarre modesty even extended to the British royal family. Whilst international protocol decrees that the ruling heads of state will recognise each other without the need for credentials, other countries issue diplomatic passports to their royal family members and some even provide a special ruling family passport such as the green leather-bound Qatari passport illustrated above.

Members of the British royal family, however, were issued with an ordinary blue passport containing the diplomatic endorsement. The document was further distinguished by the statement of the bearer's citizenship which, for example in the case of His Royal Highness Prince Charles was: 'Prince of the Royal House'. A little different from the common, 'British Subject, Citizen of the UK and Colonies'.

In order to conform to the format of the standard European Union passport, Britain brought in a diplomatic passport in 1999.

Although Great Britain did not produce a diplomatic passport, it did use a passport which carried the word *diplomatique* endorsed on the cover – the passport still issued to the Queen's Messenger. The number of Queen's Messengers varies generally between twenty and thirty at any one time and the posts are offered to senior-ranking army officers upon retirement. The position requires them to accompany the diplomatic bag as it travels from one diplomatic post to another. Only certain diplomatic bags are accompanied; the selection depends upon the route the bag is to follow. If the bag can be entrusted to a national airline then it travels unaccompanied and is met by an embassy official upon arrival. In some areas of the globe, such as parts of South America and Eastern Asia, there is no British carrier available and that is where the Queen's Messenger shows his worth. One must not be lulled into thinking that all that is required of him is to be strapped to a little leather briefcase and then 'jetted and ginned' around the world. The diplomatic bag is most likely to be in the form of several weighty mail bags and on some journeys they have to accompany him in the passenger cabin, sitting on the seats next to him and for which he holds the tickets.

The Messenger system developed from the feudal obligations which existed in King Henry II's time. Tenants were obliged to carry their lord's letters for a stated number of days per year or for a certain distance at all times of the year. By 1209 there was in existence a messenger service for King John and his court, financed by the Chancery. As the Messengers were employed by the Chancery they could be obliged not only to deliver letters but also to serve summonses from the King upon his unfortunate subjects, supervise the security and running of the Royal Household when it took to the road, look after animals or prisoners and baggage and on certain occasions, to carry money abroad to pay for the King's wars.

Over the centuries this latter obligation expanded such that by 1772 there existed in London a Corps of King's Foreign Service Messengers which had carved itself a distinction from the 'domestic' messenger service. The number of King's Messengers employed at any one time has varied through the years. In 1824 the number was increased from thirty to thirty eight yet by the outbreak of the First World War, their number had dwindled to six.

The Queen's Messenger's passport is not a diplomatic passport. The holder does not have diplomatic status and yet it brazenly carries the phrase *Courrier Diplomatique* in French on its cover. This was as a result of a ruse suggested in August 1940 by an employee of the Foreign Office by the name of Mr L. Dunlop. It was his task to revise the draft of the King's Messenger passport, get it approved by his superior and then re-order from the printers. After having made a few corrections to the French text he suggested:

> It is most important that our KMs [King's Messengers] should have every possible facility when travelling. The present passport is recognised and let us hope – respected by British authorities but foreign passport controllers are not so ready to be forthcoming. The word 'diplomatic' of course impresses them and I think it would be useful if it appeared in its French form on the cover of the KM's passport. I would suggest therefore that the wording on the front cover should be revised.... This I am sure will have the desired effect without in any way raising our old friend the question of issuing diplomatic passports.[2]

Dunlop's suggestion was approved, incorporated in the new issue and continues to successfully fool foreign border controls today as it has done for the last sixty years. The reluctance of the Foreign Office to introduce a diplomatic passport was fuelled by the worry that every MP would demand one and the Foreign Office believed diplomacy to be outside the remit of members of Parliament.[3]

The special red passport issued to the Queen's Messenger, 1984.

Although it carries the word 'diplomatique' on its cover, it is not a diplomatic passport. This was a trick invented by a civil servant to try to facilitate the Messenger's journeys.

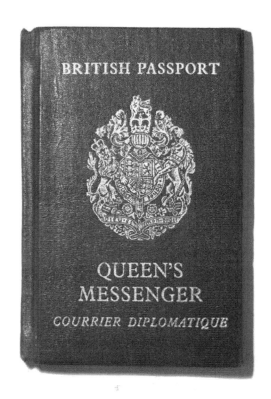

Sometimes a civilian passing through a country is entreated by his local government representative to carry some mail from one embassy to another. He does not become a Queen's Messenger but is issued with an extra passport, a Courier's Passport, to accompany his British passport and facilitate his passage just for this one journey.

In October 1940, the British radio commentator and journalist, Richard Dimbleby was issued with one such passport to carry the diplomatic mail from Cairo in Egypt to Ankara in Turkey. The large sheet with the impressive red crest at the top, accompanied by the diplomatic visas which had been endorsed in his ordinary British passport served to pass him through Syria. At that time Syria was closed to civilians for it was a French Mandated Territory

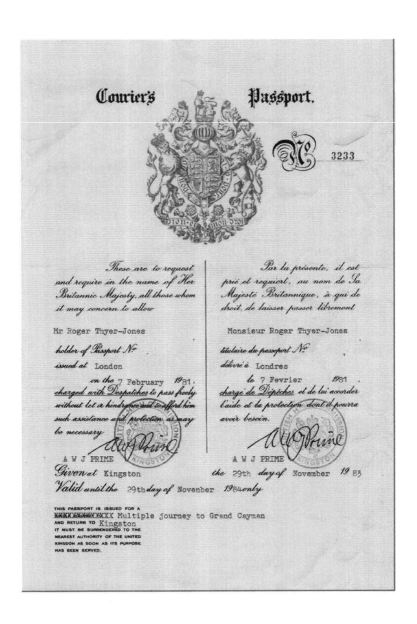

A British passport issued in 1983 to a 'courier charged with despatches'.

and France had already signed an armistice with Germany. Dimbleby was effectively entering enemy territory.[4]

The next grade down from the diplomatic passport is the special or service passport. Some countries reserve this for consular officers who do not enjoy diplomatic status, others issue both service and special passports. They might go to high-ranking members of the armed forces or to all civil servants, which in Turkey includes schoolteachers and in Afghanistan, students going to study abroad. The Spanish *Especial Pasaporte* current in the 1970s was actually only issued to persons who were stateless. Some countries further distinguish their citizens with Ministerial passports for members of the government or even Member of Parliament passports.

One body of persons which is recognised worldwide as requiring special treatment despite its not being composed of high dignitaries or ministerial governors is that of the mercantile marine. Due to the nature of international maritime transport, it would be utterly impractical to expect a seaman to produce a passport and queue up to see a passport officer instantly and on every occasion that his ship touched land. Many cargo ships arrive at ports at which the host countries are unwilling to pay for the presence of a permanent passport officer. A ship costs the owner money all the time that it is alongside the quay and should not be delayed because of a lacuna in the system. Under international agreements, professional seamen are allowed ashore usually on the guarantee of the ship's captain by means of a shore leave pass. The identity document that a seaman carries is his Seaman's Passport. This document establishes his status of professional seaman by listing his employment history and by doing so, proves his entitlement to the exemption clauses for professional seamen which figure in most country's immigration laws.

These laws were really a recognition of a maritime tradition that had gone back centuries; while passengers had passports, the crew had their ship to guarantee them. In the early twentieth century a new breed of international worker came into being – the airline pilot and his crew. To cope with the requirements of this new industry, the maritime law was adapted. As a result, aircraft have red and green navigation lights and carry 'ship's papers'. It would be unfairly onerous to expect a member of an airline crew to show his or her passport every time that the aircraft landed and so international air agreements have been negotiated to allow the crew to travel without passports provided that they carry their pilot's licence or airline crew certificate with them. In most countries this will also allow them to leave the airport and visit nearby cities.

One of the most widely used of the non-ordinary passports is, strictly speaking, not a passport at all. The stateless Travel Document was introduced by the International Refugee Organisation in 1946 to replace the Nansen Passport which was no longer issued after the dissolution of the League of Nations. This document aimed to provide a recognisable form of identity to displaced persons who were unable to obtain national travel papers. Under the agreement of 15 October 1946, the signatory countries undertook to print a guarantee that the holder would be re-admitted to the country issuing it if he returned within a stated time limit. Once again the problem of persons in the wrong place and unable to move across frontiers was having to be addressed. The travel document, although issued by individual countries did not give the holder the nationality of that country and it stated quite clearly on its first page: 'The holder of this document is the concern of the International Refugee Organisation'.

To ensure that this document would not be mistaken for a national passport it was given a pale-green cover with two black lines running diagonally across its left corner. The IRO was a body of the United Nations Organisation and was replaced in 1952 by the United Nations High

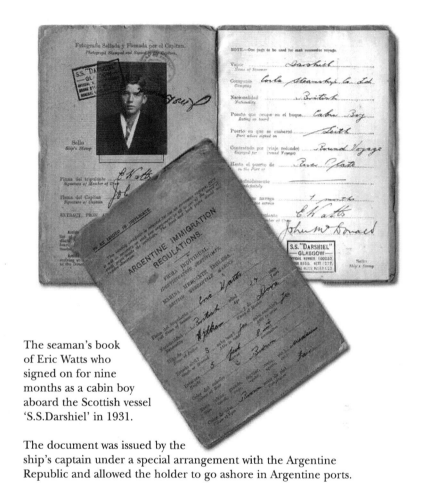

The seaman's book of Eric Watts who signed on for nine months as a cabin boy aboard the Scottish vessel 'S.S.Darshiel' in 1931.

The document was issued by the ship's captain under a special arrangement with the Argentine Republic and allowed the holder to go ashore in Argentine ports.

Commissioner's Office for Refugees (UNHCR). One of the aims of this office was to campaign for countries to give their citizenship to the children of stateless persons born on their soil. This was essential if the numbers of such people were to be reduced. Under its auspices the Geneva Convention Relating to the Status of Refugees was agreed on 28 July 1951 and the stateless travel document changed to blue, still with the characteristic black diagonal lines but with no indication that the holder was the concern of anybody other than the state in which he resided.

This was fine if one were stateless and a refugee but it did not cover those who were not refugees but were still unable to obtain a national document. As a result, in 1954 a third convention was signed and another document was invented, having a bright-pink cover and no diagonal lines. The purpose of all these conventions was to assimilate the stateless nationals into a country and eventually to obtain that nationality for them. Paradoxically, some holders of the pink travel document had been rendered stateless by the very country which had issued the document to them. In the Netherlands, for example, certain persons who had fought on the 'wrong' side during the Second World War were deprived of their Dutch citizenship in 1945. Having no entitlement to any other country's citizenship, they became stateless.

The first draft of a covenant of the League of Nations had been drawn up by the American president Woodrow Wilson in 1919 and yet, the USA refused to join the League. The Headquarters of the United Nations is in New York but the USA is not a signatory to the Geneva convention of 1951 nor indeed to the New York Convention of 1954. It is under the directions of these two agreements that most of the world's refugees have been documented. A stateless person resident in the USA who wishes to travel cannot avail himself of the visa-free agreement which obtains in most of Western Europe; he has to arm himself with a white booklet entitled 'Permit to Re-enter the United States' and obtain the necessary visas from the countries he intends to visit.

Over the years, documents for refugees have provided some intriguing non-ordinary passports. In July 1940, the remnants of the British Army escaped through a northern French port called Dunkirk and France was effectively defeated. The French Government moved south to the

Part of a travel order countersigned by the French Vichy government requesting the Germans to allow a Belgian to pass through Occupied France, 16 July 1940.

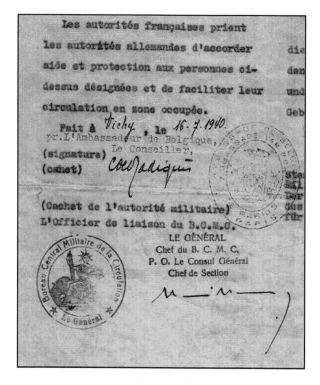

town of Vichy and there it signed an armistice with the invading Germans. France was divided into an occupied zone and an unoccupied zone. Amidst all this confusion a Belgian lady civilian wished to return home to Brussels. One of the first acts of the new government was to close all its borders to civilians of Belgium, Holland and Luxembourg so the Belgian Consul issued letters to his compatriots implying that they were embassy officials required in Belgium on urgent government business. It was then up to the individual's ingenuity and persuasiveness to do the rest. She succeeded in getting her service orders (picured above) countersigned by the Vichy Government and made her way home. The bizarreness of the power-sharing situation is indicated by the paragraph in which the vanquished French authorities beg the victorious German authorities to allow her to pass through Occupied France.

We have already seen that refugees, although a modern day preoccupation, are not a recent phenomenon and officials have been trying to find ways of dealing with them for centuries. In January 1826 a penniless Spanish refugee named François Hortel disembarked in the French port of Marseille carrying a passport issued to him by the police in Barcelona and addressed to the French Interior Minister. He was claiming asylum. The Prefect of the Département of the Bouches du Rhone of which Marseille was the capital saw his duty plain and clear. The passport was to be forwarded directly to Paris where the claim for asylum would be considered by the Minister and the decision then communicated to him. He could easily predict the outcome for Article 120 of the Constitution stated: 'The French people give asylum to foreigners banned from their own country, in the cause of liberty. It refuses it to tyrants.'

It was possible that this did not suit the Prefect. He knew that if Hortel were granted asylum then he would fall a charge on the Poor Rates of the city of Marseille and they would have to feed and lodge him. Maybe he looked for a solution that would be more amenable to the good citizens of Marseille. He found it in the Internal Passport. A passport for travelling abroad at that time could only be issued on the authority of the Minister of the Interior in Paris and the Prefect perhaps preferred to keep this gentleman in ignorance of the existence of Hortel. Instead of forwarding the Barcelona passport to the Minister, he went to his cupboard and selected a passport form of a type that he knew he was authorised to issue locally without reference to Paris. It was an Internal Passport for a Destitute Person and he altered it to read, 'Valid for overseas travel'. He then issued it to Hortel on the following terms:

A French internal passport, issued in 1826. It was altered
to permit a Spanish refugee to go to London.

We invite the civil and military authorities to allow to freely
pass from Marseille, département of the Bouches du Rhone to
London via Calais the named HORTEL François, Spanish
refugee, of whom it is entreated that he leave Marseille within
three days counting from today and not to stop anywhere in
France; to not leave the route listed overleaf and to get
himself to Calais within forty days where he will present
himself to the authorities upon arrival.

And just to make it perfectly clear, on the reverse of the
passport was inscribed the list of towns through which he
had to pass: 'Aix, Lanibere, Orgon, Avignon, Montélimar,
Valence, Lyon, Macon, Chalon sur Saone, Dijon, Chatillon
sur Seine, Troyes, Chalons sur Marne, Reims, Laon, La
Fère, Péronne, Arras, Béthune, Aire sur Lys et Calais'.

Whether Hortel expressed a wish to travel to England or
whether it was an arbitrary decision on the behalf of French
officialdom will have to remain one of life's little mysteries.

It was no mystery why Mr Sol Gareth Davis came to England from the USA in January 1953, for he told the immigration officer that he was passing through on his way to India. The officer endorsed his document with a stamp allowing him to stay for three months without taking employment. Unfortunately, Mr Davis did not go to India but overstayed his immigration permission. On 10 May he was discovered camped under one of the stands which had been erected opposite Buckingham Palace in preparation for the Coronation of Queen Elizabeth II. When the constable told him to go to one of the shelters for the homeless he refused so he was arrested. He was charged with 'wandering abroad' and remanded in custody for a week. At Bow Street Magistrates' Court he refused to plead, saying that he wanted to stay in London to see the Coronation. He said that he had twice sent a petition to the Queen to ask permission to stay longer than the stamp in his passport would allow him. He was conditionally discharged and given three days to leave Britain on the P&O liner *Stratheden* for Bombay. The day after the ship's departure from the port of Tilbury, just outside London, Mr Davis was seen in Fleet Street and arrested again. He declared himself to be 'World Citizen Number One'. This declaration did not prevent him from being deported back to the USA, nor did it prevent him from being refused entry to Britain at Southampton in the following year.

Despite ridicule, Mr Davis took his World Citizenship seriously enough to issue his own passports and started a trend that was to blossom worldwide. Garry Davis invented a fictional organisation called 'The World Service Authority, Basle, Switzerland' its name being gold blocked onto the blue cover of his 'passport'. With its thirty-two pages, the holder's photograph and a text printed in five languages, the document was sufficiently similar to a genuine passport that the border-control officers of some countries mistakenly endorsed it.

This is not a passport at all – the World Service Authority is a fictive organisation.

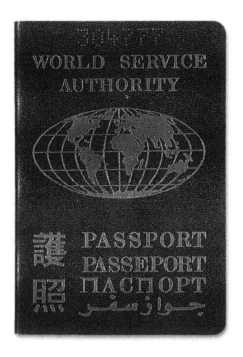

Once Garry Davis had shown the world the possibilities, his idea was copied by others. An Italian called Bruno Fabbri declared in 1963 that his bedsit in Zurich was extra-terrestrial territory and named it 'The Republic of Koneuwe'. This apparently stood for 'Communist, Neutral, Western'. He then issued some very high quality passports, both ordinary and diplomatic, and sold them to applicants. He was not alone. An untraced source, believed to have been in the Netherlands, would issue an impressive maroon-covered passport in the name of the 'Service d'information Code Diplomatique et Consulaise.'

Occasionally such spurious passports have been made for political ends, usually to promote self-determination of a minority group or at least raise its profile in the world's consciousness. Thus we have seen the Welsh passport –

Wales is part of the United Kingdom and does not issue its own passports – and the Catalan passport – Catalonia is an old Spanish principality which has now given its name to the region around Barcelona and it is an integral part of Spain.

Fifty years later, Garry Davis' initiative has been fully extended by commercial enterprises which will provide their customers with a 'camouflage' passport issued to a high standard and sometimes accompanied by additional identity cards such as a driving licence or hunting licence. The documents differ from those already mentioned in that they are not issued in the name of fictitious countries but in the former name of a country which has changed its name, such as Rhodesia (now Zimbabwe) or Burma (Myanmar) and are accompanied by a service to update visa and entry and exit stamps free of charge every two or three years. The purpose is to enable the holder to establish a credible alternative nationality and identity so that in the terrorist hijack or kidnapping situation, they can appear as a low-profile, non-interest individual; a factor which could save their life.

None of these spurious passports are forgeries of an original document, they are pure fantasy. In issuing the documents no actual crime is being committed. Persons attempting to use them for travel either succeed, in which case it proves itself by its function to be a passport, or they fail and are dealt with under the relevant country's immigration laws.

Inevitably, one group of persons who are attracted to the acquisition of such documents are those who, for any reason, are unable to obtain a passport. Another group would be those wishing to perhaps commit crimes or flee justice. But spurious or fantasy documents are not the only resource utilised by such persons.

10

AND HERE'S ONE I MADE EARLIER

When the two Austrian detectives burst into the lodging room in downtown Vienna in June 1922, they were certain that finally they had run to ground the mysterious Frenchman they had been pursuing. The Gendarmerie had been tracking him throughout Austria for nearly a month and on several occasions had lost trace of him entirely. Now, confronted by the two policemen, he fought like a madman. They were unprepared for the ferocity of his resistance for he had looked such a mild-mannered person. He lashed out, he kicked, he bit. The three men crashed about the room in their struggle, upsetting furniture and cannoning into the woodwork. At the sound of the commotion and unaware of its cause, the neighbours sent for the police and it was only when reinforcements arrived that the man was eventually overpowered and handcuffed. Even then the story was not over for in an unguarded moment he pulled a white pill from a pocket in his waistcoat and swallowed it. He was rushed out to a first aid station to have his stomach pumped and then taken to a secure hospital to recover. There he was charged with resisting arrest and failing to register with the police, but these were merely holding charges to allow the time for the extradition procedure to be set to work.

The man detained held a French passport in the name of Louis Vernier which had been issued in Lille on 29 May 1919 to enable the holder to travel to Ireland. Perhaps he had. What was certain was that the man now in possession of the passport was not Vernier, for the passport had been forged. His name was Bevan and he was English. The French passport of the time was only valid for one year and so he had altered the date of issue to read '1922'. For the photograph, he had simply pasted a photograph of himself over the original of Vernier and forged the endorsing stamp over the image to make it appear genuine. Why had he done it? What was he running from?

Gerald Lee Bevan had been, until the February of 1922, the senior partner in the second-oldest established firm of stockbrokers trading in the City of London and the chairman of the City Equitable Fire Insurance Company. It was when the shares of the latter company crashed in value in January 1922 that the trouble started and questions began to be asked. The day that the Official Receiver was sent in to liquidate the company, Bevan announced that he had been advised to go abroad on medical advice. Indeed, he found the advice so pressing that rather than take the Folkestone Packet to the continent, he flew direct to Paris. When the full state of affairs regarding the finances of his company was known, a warrant was issued for his arrest.

No trace was found of him until two weeks later when he appeared in Naples and applied for a visa for Constantinople at the Spanish Consulate. They told him to go to the British Consulate. The British Consul politely apologised but informed Bevan that he had received orders to impound his passport and did so. Luckily for Bevan, the orders which had come from the British Embassy in Rome gave no explanation for the reason and the Consul allowed Bevan to depart. By the time that the second and third telegrams had arrived, instructing the Consul first to have Bevan followed and then to have him arrested, not surprisingly, Bevan could not be found.

Bevan disappeared from sight until the Salzburg Gendarmerie notified Vienna that a suspicious Frenchman had been living there with two lady companions. They were ordered to investigate but in the meantime Bevan had decided that Salzburg attracted too many English people and he risked being recognised and so he had left. He was next seen in Innsbruck on 3 May, attempting to change 26 million Austrian crowns into German marks in order to go to Munich. Although this sum only amounted to £600, it was remarked because generally foreigners only changed small amounts at a time because the exchange rate was improving always in their favour and they stood to gain more by waiting. He failed in this transaction and by the time he returned to Salzburg he must have realised he was being followed for he went into a bank and whilst the detective waited outside for him to reappear, he left by another door.[1]

Justice finally caught up with Bevan and he was extradited to Britain to face the charge of fraud, but his case illustrated the apparent ease with which dishonest persons could turn to forgery. It was never discovered how he had acquired the French passport and although the alterations he had perpetrated upon it were ridiculed afterwards by the authorities as 'clumsy' or 'obvious', when they were coupled with his command of French they had proved themselves convincing enough to prevent the police from arresting him on several occasions.

The attitude of the travelling public to the passport has long been to consider it as a nuisance rather than a facility. This is understandable since, as Napoleon III observed, the passport never stops the criminal it merely obstructs the free passage of the innocent. However, the latter are not always as innocent as one would expect. The diarist, John Evelyn, in recounting some difficulties he encountered on a journey to Paris in 1650, freely admits to having forged documents: 'Sat out for Paris, taking post at Gravesend, and so that night to Canterbury where being surpriz'd by the souldiers, and having only an antiquated passe, with some fortunate dexterity I got cleare of them, tho' not without extraordinary hazard, having before counterfeited one with successe...'[2]

The falsifying or misuse of such documents by otherwise honest persons seems to have been quite acceptable – an attitude rather akin to that of the modern tourist who will try to smuggle a few extra cigarettes or some other contraband through a customs control. It is not seen as really dishonest, more a sort of sport. Such an attitude often generates an outrage of disbelief by the perpetrator when caught red-handed.

If a document exists which confers favour or advantage on its owner, then somebody will take the trouble to forge it. The difference between 'counterfeiting' and 'forging' is that counterfeiting is the complete manufacture of an imitation original whereas forging is the altering of a previously genuine article. Thus a genuine passport where somebody has altered the name and changed the photograph is forged; a passport which has been printed, assembled and bound to imitate a genuine article, is counterfeit.

For the same reasons that the counterfeiting of currency is not publicised, so the falsification of passports is hushed up. One must do everything to retain public faith. If it becomes widely known that your country's passport is easily forged and has been used by unentitled persons then the genuine holders of such passports will possibly find themselves subject to undue scrutiny at border crossings and the prestige of the country will suffer. When cases of passport forgery come to court the defendant usually pleads guilty and so material proof of the forgery is not demanded. Should the defence counsel challenge the prosecution to prove that the passport is forged then the court generally goes in camera and so the details are never released. Passport forgery is not a subject easily researched by the layman.

The USA has divulged that between 1914 and 1945 three complete counterfeit versions of their red-covered passport were detected,[3] and it is known that the British 'perfection itself' passport was counterfeited within five years of its introduction. This was discovered because the counterfeit passport had a spelling mistake on the royal arms on the front cover *'Dieu et mon drou'* instead of *'Dieu et mon droit',* the pages were thinner than on the genuine one and the revenue stamp affixed on the inside front cover was smooth instead of embossed.

At least three counterfeit versions of the USA red passport (left) were discovered in the period extending from the beginning of the First World War to the end of the Second and counterfeit examples of the beige Belgian A series passport (right) were used by Communist agitators in China in the 1930s.

False passports can be used by various persons: spies, criminals, terrorists, immigrants, refugees, and each for a different reason. The intended use of the document will influence the choice of passport to forge and the quality of workmanship required. In order to cash stolen travellers' cheques, for example, the thief would enter the name and personal details of the owner of the cheques into a blank counterfeit document, but with his own photograph affixed in it. He would then travel on his own passport to a country whose bank clerks would be unfamiliar with the genuine version of his counterfeit passport and there, cash the cheques, having practised the signature beforehand and now proving his identity with the false document. The standard of forgery required in this type of passport is only of that necessary to dupe a bank clerk. This is no condemnation of the percipience of bank clerks but rather an illustration of how specialised knowledge can cover a narrow spectrum. Thus a bank clerk might accept an Italian identity card that a passport officer would laugh at while a passport officer might not demur at dollar bills whose patent spuriousness would give the bank clerk apoplexy.

Terrorists might need a passport of a country whose nationals are not usually linked with terrorism, since the border controls might be paying particular attention to certain nationalities in an effort to foil a suspected terrorist plot. The choice of which country's passport to counterfeit is influenced by several factors, not the least of which is the racial group of the intended users. Trying to ensure an easy passage by copying a passport of a respected and peaceable nation such as Sweden or Switzerland is probably not a workable idea if the terrorist users are likely to be of a Mediterranean or Arabic appearance. Although many nations now have a wide racial mix in them, giving a terrorist a passport in the identity of an unusual minority group will serve to make him prominent not discreet.

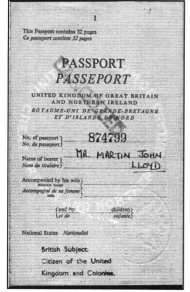 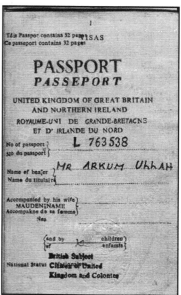

On the left is a page from a genuine British passport issued in 1965. On the right is the same page from a counterfeit example. The forger has used a visa page from a genuine passport but has omitted to erase the word 'visas' at the top. Note also the mixture of French and English within the same line and the general uneven quality of printing.

Over the years counterfeit passports discovered in the possession of terrorists have purported to have come from many different countries such as Bahrein, Morocco, Cyprus and Nicaragua. In the early 1930s, Communist agitators in China were found to be documented with false versions of the Belgian A series passport. They presumably hoped that the country's well known neutrality would coat them with a layer of innocuousness.

Another technique used by terrorists and criminals alike is to steal unissued passports which can then be used for whoever and whenever one desires. The risk in trying to purloin the passports from the printers is that they may not be wholly manufactured on one site and half-finished passports introduce unwelcome risks. Any attempt to procure the materials necessary to finish them would attract the attention of a police force already aware of what you are seeking. The preferred method is to raid the issuing office itself and the best countries to raid are those where the passport issue is decentralised such as the Netherlands or Belgium. Here you can burgle a town hall and not only steal a few hundred blank passports but also the stamps and seals necessary to authenticate their issue. Some of the blank German passports stolen from the Town Hall at Hessen in 1971 by Ulrike Meinhof, of the notorious Baader-Meinhof gang, were later to turn up in the hands of the PFLP. Among the belongings of Ilich Ramirez Sanchez, better known as the terrorist 'Carlos', was a handstamp for authenticating the photographs in British passports.[4] It has been suggested in official circles that the suicide crews involved in the terrorist attack on the World Trade Centre in New York on 11 September 2001, had travelled through Europe on stolen blank Belgian passports.

In any one year, thousands of blank passports go missing worldwide. Each time one reads of an embassy being sacked during a civil uprising it is almost certain that the consular section would have been afforded special attention. Less spectacular but more insidious is the theft from within the embassy by locally employed staff. This sometimes does not come to light until an audit reveals the deficit, and the issue of passports in some consular offices is of such a desultory nature that it is impossible to state with any authority upon what date the passports 'went missing'.

In some cases the passports are brazenly given directly to a terrorist organisation by an indulgent government. Western countries sometimes accuse Arabic countries such as Iraq and Algeria of fostering terrorism by issuing their own passports to persons not entitled to them. Can one be certain that Western countries are not doing likewise?

One problem a terrorist may have to face is concealing details of his movements. He may wish to erase from his passport evidence of having travelled to countries of a certain political persuasion or which are known to train terrorists. An established technique is to remove and replace the offending pages with blank ones from another passport. The so called 'shoe bomber', Richard Reid, who allegedly attempted to blow up American Airlines flight 63 from Paris to Miami on 22 December 2001 by detonating explosives which had been packed into the heel of his shoe, had managed to conceal his previous movements with the unwitting help of the British Consulate in Amsterdam. He is reported to have deliberately put his passport into the washing machine. This act loosened the Pakistani visa sticker and he was able to peel it from the document, leaving no trace of its removal. He then applied at the Consulate for a replacement passport. This was issued to him four days later and, of course, carried no trace of his previous travels.[5]

An intending immigrant sometimes requires the reverse of this service. He might wish for particular pages to be put into his passport. These would probably have been removed from another passport and would perhaps carry a visa which would gain him entry to the country of his choice or the pages may carry a series of border stamps to indicate that he was a regular traveller when in fact he had never visited the country before. When the demand is sufficient, he might even purchase an entire counterfeit passport.

Modern-day refugees will use any document they can in order to get on board the aeroplane, ship or train taking them to their preferred destination. This is made easier by the attitude of some countries towards their own embarkation control. Whatever is discovered to be wrong with the individual or his passport, its importance is qualified by the fact that he is leaving the country and not entering it. He is thus more likely to become a problem for

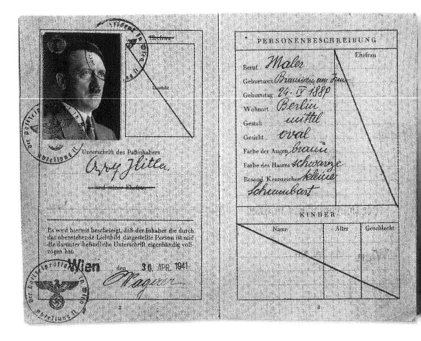

A counterfeit produced by the forgery section of the British SOE during the Second World War. This group was formed partly from convicted forgers who were released from prison for war work. Their job was to manufacture all kinds of identity documents needed by the SOE agents in Occupied Europe – a task they enlivened by the occasional joke such as this. The letter J on the front page is in red ink and denotes that Hitler is Jewish.

the country of destination. Once on board, the technique is then for the refugee to utterly destroy the document, flushing it down the plane toilet or throwing it over the ship's rail so that on arrival he can claim asylum in whatever nationality and identity will ensure that he is not returned directly whence he came.

Although instances of forgery have surfaced in the last two hundred years, for much of this time there was little point in forging a passport. In many circumstances they were not required and the border control was such that it would have been less trouble to simply take the risk of travelling without a passport than to try to alter or counterfeit one. Early passports, as we have seen in the case of Orsini, did not need to be altered to be misused. Instead of forging the document, you forged the holder. However, there could be unforseen risks in adopting the identity or name of another.

In 1824, an Italian, Edmond Angellini appealed to the Lord Mayor of London for assistance. He had travelled Europe as an itinerant translator for various literary journals and had been engaged as tutor to Lady Oxford and her family in Rouen. Upon leaving her employment he decided to improve his prospects by travelling to London.

When he came to this country, he took the liberty of using her ladyship's name and it was written upon his passport... he found, however, after such delay in England as gave a full opportunity for experiment that the market for the kind of talent he possessed was glutted and that the most respectfully educated and introduced emigrants were teaching languages at 18d. per lesson.... in such a discouraging state of things he was desirous of returning to Venice and accordingly applied to the Austrian Ambassador for a passport, This he was refused. ... He had since been informed to his great surprise, that Lady Oxford, whose name was on the passport, was one of a number of eminent persons who were much feared by Austria, and prohibited from entering the Austrian dominions.[6]

Signor Angellini discovered that making an assumption on the probity of the person whose name he intended to adopt, could be a treacherous economy.

In 1858, Mr Featherstonhaugh, the British Consul in Le Havre, succinctly described his technique for detecting impostors when recounting a passport application recently made to him: 'I invariably examine every person and I found his appearance was not that of an Englishman. I generally know an Englishman and it is difficult to deceive me...'[7] The unfortunate applicant in question, claimed to have been born in York but did not know of any big churches there and had never heard of York Minster. This was not surprising because he later admitted that he was Russian.

The authorities issuing the documents were not blind to events and took whatever measures they could to prevent the debasing of their passes. One of the cheapest and most effective safeguards against forgery was to issue passports only on official watermarked paper which was not available commercially. A watermark is a design which is introduced into the filament of the paper at the manufacturing stage by passing the raw wet paper between two rollers upon which the chosen design has been moulded in relief. This causes the paper to stretch and thin at certain points and thus allow more light to pass through than through the surrounding fibres. The design does not interfere with whatever is to be printed on the paper for it is invisible in normal light; it is only when light passes through the paper, such as when the document is held up before a window, that the watermark is distinguishable. Watermarks were probably used originally as a trade mark by the paper manufacturer, to reassure the buyer that he was purchasing the genuine article. For the purposes of security, it was a simple commercial operation to ensure that the paper reserved for the exclusive use of the government bore a distinctive and unique watermark.

Security watermark on a French passport of 1808.

It consists of a portrait of the Emperor, encircled with the inscription, 'Napoléon I Empéreur des Français'.

The French were exploiting the properties of the watermark as a security feature in the eighteenth century. All paper destined for passports was watermarked with a central motif. This sometimes depicted the monarch, sometimes the National Printing Works but it always carried top and bottom the description of the document, 'External passport' for example. Despite the security offered by watermarks, many European principalities and kingdoms were not using them on passports even as late as the nineteenth century. Britain did not begin to issue security watermarked passports until the twentieth century although some nineteenth-century passports were printed on paper bearing the papermaker's commercial watermark.

The watermark is in widespread use today and still provides counterfeiters with the thorny problem of whether to ignore the mark or try to imitate it and if the latter, how.

Crisp, detailed embossing on a
Saxon passport of 1854

Poor definition embossing
American passport of 19

Attempts have been made to forge a watermark by applying solvents to the paper to thin it where required and for a while a certain amount of success was achieved by splitting the paper and painting in a watermark with white paint and then re-pasting the paper together. Although one of the earliest security devices adopted, the watermark remains one of the more difficult to forge.

Along with the adoption of the watermark came the blind embossing stamp. This is manufactured by casting a design in relief on a block of steel and a recessed mirror image in an opposite block. When a document is placed between the male and female dies and the two pressed together, the intricate design is embossed into the fibres of the paper. This is a characteristic which is very difficult to imitate without great expense. It was employed initially to validate a document. Validation was needed because once the pre-printed forms had been introduced, a person stealing a form could, with but a little effort, issue himself a passport. Authenticating the document with a blind embossing introduced another hurdle. The press itself is a heavy piece of equipment – it would have been bolted to a bench and padlocked when not in use. The grace and execution of some nineteenth century embossings is breathtaking – the modern ones, less so. Great Britain used an embossed stamp in the nineteenth century to record that the stamp duty on the passport form had been paid.

The blind embossing stamp really came into its own once the authorities began to insist on photographs for their passports. Now the embossing could pass through the paper and the image, tying the two together and making any alteration difficult because the replacement picture would have to bear the exact imprint. The forgers tackled this problem in several ways. As many countries had standardised on a circular stamp as being the most efficient and long lasting, in some cases the forger was able to select a photograph taken from a genuinely issued passport and align the sector of the circle up with the part remaining on the page and hope that the radius was roughly correct. Circular dry embossing stamps were available commercially and as only one corner of the photograph was usually stamped, whether that quarter of the stamp bore the correct design or not could be overlooked. In this they were assisted by two factors: the mediocre standard of some official embossing stamps which should have been replaced when they had become worn but for reasons of economy were not; and the variable skills displayed by the staff issuing the passports.

When a pre-embossed photograph was not available, a tracing was taken of that portion of the stamp which should appear on the photograph and this was then applied to the back of the false photograph and embossed through it with the aid of a ball-point pen. Clever forgers used a pen with no ink in. The result was not as crisp as an original but was still a passable image. Unfortunately, a modification introduced by some countries in the 1970s to make photograph substitution by this method more difficult, had the reverse effect. A self-adhesive clear plastic film was laid across the photograph and page before embossing. Once the forgers had discovered how to remove the film without damaging the page, they realised that the plastic film retained a sharp impression of the stamp and all that was needed was to lay it back over the new photograph.

In the nineteenth century the qualities looked for in paper chosen for passports were its ability to take a good, detailed impression; its resistance to wear and its impressive 'feel'. However, these qualities did not necessarily ensure a secure passport – the harder the paper the easier it was to make an alteration without disturbing the fibres.

Once the change had been made to the book-form passport in the 1920s it was found that the hardness and

Latent image in a Lithuanian passport, 1992.
Above, when viewed flat, only the geometrical design is visible.
Below, when viewed from an oblique angle, the word 'Letuva',
(Lithuania) becomes apparent.

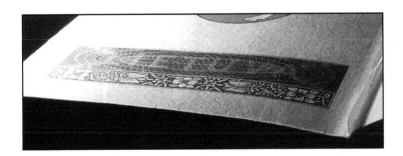

sizing of the paper could be reduced because the paper did not need to be self-supporting as was necessary when it had been a single folded sheet. The document was now protected from abrasion by strong covers. Not only was this paper cheaper to produce but it showed up unauthorised amendments more readily. In order to highlight further any attempted alteration, the pages were printed with a background print of fine lettering designed to make photographic reproduction difficult. Also, a special ink was used which dispersed when made wet. Any attempt at bleaching or washing out the written entries in the passport would thus result in the surrounding ink running into a stain. 'Fugitive ink', as it was called, was refined by the addition of secret reagents which would react with the preferred chemicals of the forger and turn the stain a contrasting colour.

The principle of printing the background of the page in fugitive and reactive ink has been continued to this day to the point where the ink under the clear plastic laminate on the personal details page of a passport will now react when it comes into contact with oxygen, thus indicating any attempts at lifting the layer in order to alter the details underneath.

Another use of distinctive ink is the inclusion at some location in the document of a complicated ornamental design printed by the intaglio process. This method leaves the ink as a relief coating on the paper rather than as an impression in the paper. It is more expensive to achieve than straightforward lithography and this is an important security factor because counterfeiters rarely have access to the same technologies as the printer and so have to imitate. They would normally try to reproduce an original intaglio-printed design by photolithography, which would give a reasonably accurate image but would not stand proud of the page as would intaglio printing. A passport-checker who doubts the authenticity of the document only has to discreetly pass a thumb or fingertip across an area of supposed intaglio printing and if it feels smooth then it is a forgery.

This quality of intaglio printing, that of producing a raised image on the paper, has been further extended in the ghost or latent image. Here, an intricate design is printed in intaglio, often on the inside of the cover but in making the printing plate a second image is cut across it at an angle in such a manner that when printed it does not run deeply enough to be immediately apparent. If the viewpoint is taken at a position almost level with the surface of the paper, the second image appears.

The ability to place a secret mark in a passport, only visible to the initiated, must have been a tantalising goal for passport-issuing authorities. In the 1930s the Russians succeeded in marking particular pages of the passports of certain of their own agents with symbols effected in paint which was invisible in normal (white) light but glowed when subjected to ultraviolet (UV) light. The equipment required in those days to generate a beam of ultraviolet light was bulky. Could they have imagined that one day, the ordinary citizen would be able to purchase a UV lamp which would not only be portable but would be easily carried in a handbag?

Today, the UV security safeguards in a passport are numerous and varied. A trip around one's passport with a UV lamp in a darkened room produces a phantasmagorical display of curls and whorls, numbers and words, crowns, flowers and animals in a profusion of colours. There seems to be no limit to the ingenuity employed in inventing a new safeguard. Japanese passports issued since 1 November 1999 contain a complete duplicate version of the holder's photograph which appears, ghost-like, from the middle of the details page when subjected to UV light. Here they have succeeded where the Hong Kong authorities had failed twenty years earlier. The latter were obliged to abandon the ultraviolet image in the travel documents that they issued to the stateless Chinese in their community because the special treatment applied to the paper made it crack in use.

Even seemingly innocent characteristics of a passport such as a dotted line may be not what they seem. In the 1920s the term 'microprinting' was the description given to the background print of the page which usually contained a phrase such as, in the Belgian passport for example, 'Belgie-Belgique' which was repeated in small letters hundreds of times across the page. At first glance it would merely appear as a tint but on closer inspection, the words were visible and legible to the naked eye. This was a safeguard to make photographic reproduction difficult. With improvements in photography making the copying of fine detail easier, microprinting has had to be made smaller and now requires a microscope to be distinguished.

Microprinting in a Canadian passport.

The dotted line ruled below the paragraph on 'endorsements and limitations' under high magnification reveals itself to be a repetition of the word 'CANADA'.

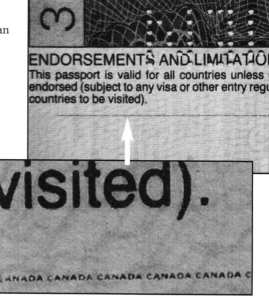

The dotted lines which divide the pages in the American passport are not dotted lines at all, they are the letters 'USA' repeated in miniature.

Recognising that eventually every document can be forged, the industry and the control authorities have concentrated on making passports of such complexity as to render any attempt at counterfeiting or falsification, financially unviable. They seem to be so certain of their infallibility that they even reveal details of these security safeguards to the public – the first page of the new issue (2000) machine-readable Belgian passport is an illustrated guide to the various anti-forgery features contained within the document.

The premise is that the level of investment and technical knowledge required to produce these security features is such that they would only be available to legitimate concerns. This does not allow for institution-sponsored forgery. In 1991 an investigation was undertaken into the commercial counterfeiting of holograms being sold to producers of pirate copies of branded consumer goods. It discovered that the source of the fake holograms was the Reflective Materials Institute of the Shenzhen University of Science and Technology in Guandong Province in China. It had manufactured 600,000 counterfeit holograms and had orders in hand for a further three million. It was fined US$ 260 by the Chinese authorities.[8] The relevance of this is that holograms had recently been adopted by states trying to increase the security of their passports.

Not many forgers are able to tap into such quasi-official resources to perpetrate their frauds and so they are forced to find a way around the expensive passport forgery. One time-tested technique is to leave the document untouched and to alter the holder to match it. This is particularly successful now that many frontier examinations focus on the technical performance of the document but afford no more than a cursory glance at the holder.

Going one stage further, it is possible to get a genuine document issued in a bogus identity by supplying the biographical details of a genuine person but with a photograph of the intended false applicant. The document thus issued will be of an apparently unimpeachable correctness; indeed, any passport officer having suspicions that the photograph has been exchanged or the details altered will be disabused by referring to the issuing office's records. The problems arise when the person whose details have already been used without his knowledge, applies for a passport and is immediately suspected of making a fraudulent application.

In November 1974, the British Labour MP Mr John Stonehouse went swimming from a Florida beach and did not return. He had left his British passport with his clothes on the sand. American coastguard and police helicopters and launches were employed to search for him but without success. During the following days, details of his political and business life enlivened the mystery. Had he really been a spy for Czechoslovakia? Were his trading companies in financial difficulties? By Christmas, Mr Stonehouse had turned up in Australia as Dr Joseph Arthur Markham. When arrested by the Melbourne police as a suspected illegal immigrant he claimed that he had been blackmailed and had decided to start again in a new identity. In order to do so he had applied for a British passport in the identity of a person whom he knew to be dead.

This was a technique which had been made famous in the contemporary work of fiction *The Day of the Jackal.* In this thriller, the main character had searched a churchyard to find the grave of a young child. Supplied with the information from the headstone – name of child, age, date of death, names of the parents, – he could now go to the Registrar General's Office and obtain a copy of the child's birth certificate. This was a service available to all citizens upon payment of a small fee. A birth certificate was the key

| Page 25 of an Indonesian passport viewed in white light. | The same page viewed in ultraviolet light |

documentary evidence to be submitted when applying for a passport; the character references were not routinely checked by the Passport Office and could be fabricated with no great trouble. The significance of choosing to adopt the identity of a child who had not reached adulthood was that, being a minor, it was very unlikely to have ever applied for a passport and so the fraudulent application would throw up no conflict with the records.

Stonehouse adapted this system. Using his position as an MP, he phoned up a number of London hospitals and obtained from them the details of persons who were of his approximate age and who had recently died. His attempt to change his identity failed and he was returned to the UK. Ironically, in 1960, Stonehouse had been the co-author of a work entitled *Prohibited Immigrant*.

The fraudulent passport application is not new. In the period between the two world wars, this particular kind of fraud was used extensively by Middle Eastern drug traffickers. In some countries it was even possible to obtain genuinely issued passports in a fraudulent identity by bribery or coercion of the issuing clerk.[9]

Using falsified passports can occasionally have a lighter side albeit within a tragi-comic context. In 1943, Hans Gisevius, the German Vice Consul in Switzerland, made the acquaintance of Allen Dulles of the American OSS (Office of Strategic Services). Gisevius was at that time the liaison officer for the German Resistance and was deeply involved in the plans to assassinate Hitler. When the famous plot of July 1944 failed and the officers involved had been hunted and executed, Gisevius fled to an isolated German village near the Swiss border and lay hidden there until early 1945. A Swiss friend concocted a plan to rescue him. He obtained samples of blank German passports from the German Embassy in Berne and then took them to the London office of the OSS where Dulles got permission to assist. They gave Gisevius the identity of a fictional high functionary of the Gestapo.

Then a hitch occurred. When the passport arrived in Switzerland it was noticed that one of the stamps that the OSS forgers had endorsed in it was imperfect and so it was sent back for alteration. Mindful of the fact that time was running out for Gisevius, the OSS decided to accelerate matters by giving the package to an allied officer who was returning to London by air. He arrived at the Paris airfield, tired and bruised from an uncomfortable flight and his discomfort was not in any way ameliorated by his being quizzed by a military policeman immediately his feet touched French soil. To the brusque enquiry of whether or not he was carrying papers he innocently replied, 'Only this,' and to the policeman's consternation, pulled a German Gestapo Official Passport from his pocket. [10]

But the experiences of the French General Pichegru stand as the exemplar of what awaits the unprepared user of false documents. On 4 October 1798, he disembarked from a ship called the *Amiable* at the port of Sheerness in England but he had carelessly omitted to explain to his shipboard companions that he had been travelling in the identity of 'Major Pérou'.

...I arrived here at twelve o' clock. Having alighted at the inn a sergeant came by order of the Commandant, to take me to him. We met him on the rampart and I immediately put my passport into his hands. Scarcely had he begun to read it when a naval officer of the fleet with which I had come and who had seen me on board the 'Amiable', came up to me in an affectionate manner and not content with calling me by my name, did me the attention of observing to the Commandant that he had come with me Etc. Imagine my embarrassment. But that is not all, The Commandant desired this officer to conduct me to the Admiral. I took care to inform him that I was there incognito and under another name but, not understanding French, he went on addressing me by the same and even thought it proper to publish it both to the officers we met and to the Admiral himself. After this I expect my departure will soon be known and I begin to think one ought to change one's features as well as one's name.[11]

11

Without Let or Hindrance?

The Duke of Sussex arrived in the French port of
Marseille in 1791, having come from Nice in the
Kingdom of Sardinia. When the official asked for his
passport he had to admit that he had none. He was
summarily required to present himself at the Town Hall and
apply for one. Soon the Duke found himself standing
before a municipal clerk who was bowed over the
paperwork on his desk. The clerk dipped his quill in the
ink, took a passport form and without looking up, began to
fill it in.

'What is your name?' says the clerk.
'Augustus Frederick,' replied his Royal Highness.
'No other name?'
'No.'
'Who do you belong to?'
'To my father and mother.'
'Are you of the department (county) of the Mouth of the
Rhone?'
'No sir.'
'Of what department are you?'
'Of the department of the Thames.'
'What is your father's name?'
'George.'
'What *trade* does your father follow?'
'He is King of England.'[1]

The clerk's head jerked up from his papers. He stamped and signed the form with as much gravity and dignity as he could muster. The Duke of Sussex, otherwise known as Prince Frederick Augustus, the fifth son of the reigning English monarch King George III, went away clutching his French passport which announced to all interested parties that he was, 'Mr Augustus Frederick, son of Master George of the Departement of the Thames.'

Not all passport applications were as easy as that of the Duke of Sussex. It often seemed that to travel abroad, our forefathers needed to be members of some, undefined but exclusive club. Without a passport a traveller would be delayed and hindered by various petty officials. Without letters of introduction it was unlikely that he would be admitted to the society of his class in his chosen foreign destination, but to acquire these essentials one needed to know influential people.

The seventeenth-century English poet, John Milton, when intending a voyage to Italy in 1638 had to resort to the influence of his friends and acquaintances in order to furnish himself with the necessary travel documents. He had not at that time written his most famous work, *Paradise Lost,* and his renown was not yet sufficient in his own country to serve his purpose. For letters of introduction, he turned to Sir Henry Wotton, a fellow poet but more importantly, a distinguished traveller and diplomat of the time. It is he who is remembered in diplomatic circles as having made the observation that an ambassador was 'an honest man sent to lie abroad for the good of his country'. Wotton was well aware of the usefulness of passports for he had already misused them on several occasions himself when in the service of the Earl of Essex. Employed to travel widely and collect intelligence for his master and being fluent in German and Italian, he had often passed himself off as a citizen of one or the other country as required. In 1601 for example, when sent on a secret mission from the Grand Duke of Tuscany to Scotland he had travelled with an Italian passport in the identity of Ottavio Baldi.

Wotton gave Milton letters addressed to various of his business and social contacts in France and Italy and he recommended an itinerary for him. Milton turned to another friend, Henry Lawes, who used his influence as 'musician in ordinary for the lutes and voices' of the Chapel Royal to secure Milton a passport from the Warden of the Cinque Ports. With this document Milton set out on the fifteen months of travelling in Italy which were to so influence his subsequent writings.

In some circumstances, the importance of the person issuing the passport could be somewhat compromised by the way in which it was issued. In 1789, in response to the manner in which the internal problems of France were impinging upon the way of life of the aristocracy, the Comte d'Artois made off in his carriage towards the border. His hapless valet de chambre, M. le Roux, was left to collect his master's clothes and belongings and follow on as best he could. As he bustled around the Palace of Versailles, filling his master's trunks, he saw King Louis XVI preparing to drive off to the Hotel de Ville in Paris. Gathering his courage in his hands he approached the monarch and explained that he had been bidden to follow his master, but was worried about being stopped on the road by the rabble. Could the King possibly give him a passport? The King regretted that he had no ministers with him to issue one and so could not assist him. However, seeing the man's dejected expression, he searched in a drawer and found an old passport which had already been signed by his Foreign Minister and gave him that.[2]

The class-ridden officiousness which permeated the British civil service in the nineteenth century was perhaps merely a mirror of the times but it turned applying for a passport into a judgment of the applicant's social standing.

This state of affairs was not to the liking of a reader of *The Times* in 1851:

> Sir – I have always understood, that every Englishman has a right to the protection of his Government, in any country to which he may choose to bend his steps; such, however, does not appear to be the case. Having learned, unexpectedly, on Friday last, that the packet by which I intended to proceed on my way to Poland, would sail that day, and not on Monday, as I had previously understood, I applied at the Foreign Office for a passport. I learned there, to my surprise, that before I could have one, I must obtain a recommendation to Lord Palmerston, from some M.P. or banker. Finding remonstrance useless, I proceeded in search of the representatives of my native town, neither of whom I could find. It being of great consequence to proceed immediately, I addressed a private letter to Lord Palmerston, stating the circumstances and requesting his interference. To this communication his lordship replied that 'he could only confirm the information which I appeared to have received, that no passport would be issued from the foreign department to any person who was not known to him (Lord Palmerston), or recommended by some one who was known to him.' I am thus, Sir, as far as individual inconvenience is involved, detained, by this most inquisitorial and capricious regulation, a whole week in this country, very probably to the utter destruction of the object of my journey, and most certainly to my serious injury... It appears that, unless a man be honoured with the acquaintance of my Lord Palmerston, or, at all events, with that of some happy man who is so honoured, he must either remain a prisoner for life in his native country, or go abroad exposed to the harassing and vexatious impositions of foreign governments.[3]

Even allowing for the fact that the Foreign Office issued passports on the day following the application, it would seem that if this traveller was inconvenienced by his ship departing on a Friday instead of the following Monday then he had waited until the last minute to lodge his application. The last sentence of this plaint shows that it was possible to leave the UK without a passport in 1851 – at this time, Britain did not demand passports of persons entering or leaving the country.

Even when issued, a document might not be up to the standard that one could hope to expect. The British Consul in Ragusa, (now Dubrovnik) in 1914 was Mr Hambloch. When he finally received the expected telegram from the British ambassador in Vienna, informing him that Great Britain and Austria were at war, he called on the Austrian prefect of the town and asked for his safe conduct to enable him to take a ship to Venice. He was told to return in the afternoon and it would be ready. He recounts: 'When I went to get the safe conduct in the afternoon I found it was a mean looking affair and badly typed. I asked the Prefect to correct an error in it. He did so...'[4]

Hambloch was relying upon the safe conduct to guarantee the safety of his life as he left an enemy country. Thanks to his consular experience, he had the requisite knowledge to check that the correct formula had been used and he had the authority to effect a correction. A British stockbroker living in London over eighty years later, did not need any specialist knowledge to discover that his newly issued British passport was faulty when he received it from the United Kingdom Passport Service in February 2002. The moment he opened it he knew, for there, alongside his details was the digital photograph of a complete stranger.[5]

To plead in defence that errors are inevitable is not great comfort when one considers how the modern, technically complex passport can make itself inaccessible to the layman. Few are the citizens who would be able to detect a mistake in the check code in the machine-readable text on their passport; the first indication of a mistake would be when the passport was rejected by the machine at the frontier control.

When a fault does appear in a passport, it is not always noticed before innocent people have been inconvenienced.

Variations on a Turkish passport.
Should the crescent moon face to the right or the left?
In the 1970s, nobody seemed to know.

In the late 1970s a batch of Turkish passports was printed with the star and crescent emblem laterally inverted – the star was placed on the left and the points of the crescent moon faced leftwards. The holders of these passports discovered that it was a lottery as to whether the foreign border controls would accept them or not, and the Turkish authorities were not always able to convince other countries of the authenticity of the said passports.

Astonishing but true, the authority issuing a passport is not always competent to declare whether one of their own passports presented to them is genuine or not. During the production life of a passport many minor modifications are introduced; the paper may change; the dyes used in the ink may have to be modified as a result of health and safety legislation; the background tint of the page may be altered; the entire passport contract may be awarded to a supplier who uses different binding techniques. The permutations are many and rarely is the issuing authority able to combine the production records of the individual suppliers with their own tallies of issue of documents in such a way as to define categorically the exact physical characteristics of one of their own passports issued at any one time, in any one place.

In September 1962, Box 500, a liaison section of the security service MI5, submitted a Cyprus passport to Her Majesty's Stationery Office (HMSO) to determine whether or not it was genuine. At this time, the HMSO printing works at Harrow, the paper suppliers Wiggins Teape and the printers De La Rue were in various ways involved in the production of passports for the Crown Colonies of which Cyprus was one. The investigation revealed that none of these organisations kept records on the changes in passport production but relied on members of staff who could remember or who, 'had had experience in this type of thing'. It took them until 1965 to arrive at a consensus that on balance the passport was genuine.[6]

Having secured the passport, what use is it to the holder? A hypocritical situation has long existed wherein countries, whilst respectfully requesting and requiring foreign countries to allow the bearers of their passports to pass freely without let or hindrance on the one hand, are restricting and refusing passports to their own nationals on the other hand. The usefulness of the passport as a tool of control was categorically stated in the nineteenth-century *Guide des Consulats* which declared that passports were: 'a necessary precaution to track and watch over the movements of people to assist in the administration and policing of the country.'[7]

Even Prince Louis Napoleon, who later became the assassination target of Orsini, was refused a passport by the French Ambassador in London when he was living in England in 1848. He was considered too dangerous to be allowed back into France.

It may have been a wish to exploit this quality of control that gave the world the identity card. In 1795, the French minister Mariette was struggling with the internal security problems of Paris. The revolution was in full swing; England had declared war against France two years earlier and was anxious lest the teachings and momentum of the revolution cross the Channel. In order to keep a watch on the situation, it is almost certain that English spies were circulating in the French capital and regularly reporting back to the ministry of William Pitt. Mariette proposed to bring in stricter controls on foreigners; 'The British cabinet is sowing hate amongst us... There exists in France and in Paris a crowd of foreigners over which we need more than a simple surveillance. Some of them are our sincere friends; others, our sworn enemies.'[8] By a law of 11 July 1795, he stipulated that every foreigner would have to hold a security card which carried his description. A subtle refinement was made in the design in order to assist the police when checking papers. The document would show the declaration, 'Hospitality, Security, Fraternity' – unless it had been issued to a citizen of an enemy country, in which case, 'Fraternity' would be omitted.

Freedom, Equality, Democracy or Death! – an order dated 1798 from the Commissar General Trombetta. It was written during the short-lived self-government of the Piedmontese city of Novi and addressed to the citizens of the municipality of that city, inviting them to issue passports to the four persons named below. Novi's independence lasted for about two years.

The letter of recommendation from an influential person is no longer the accepted manner of procuring a passport. The present-day applicant is confronted with forms demanding all kinds of information. What is it all used for? Is it all needed? These are questions that the ordinary citizens might rightly ask themselves. Indeed, with a little reflection, they would probably arrive at a more accurate answer than one that would be supplied by the passport-issuing authority.

And sometimes even the information that the applicant does supply is ignored, as Mr Bassett Digby complained in 1915:

> To the Editor of the Times.
> Sir – A little light might be shed, with advantage, upon the high-handed methods of the Passports Department at the Foreign Office. On the form provided for the purpose I described my face as 'intelligent'. Instead of finding this characterization entered, I have received a passport on which some official, utterly unknown to me, has taken it upon himself to call my face 'oval'.
> Yours very truly...[9]

Many application forms enquire which countries the applicant intends to visit. A British subject filling in the passport application form in 1920 would find that it demanded to know where he was travelling to and for what purpose. The official reason for this was that it enabled the Foreign Office to advise travellers of the visa requirements of their foreign destinations as indeed, it did. But that was not the entire answer. It allowed territorial restrictions to be endorsed on the passport, limiting the area of permitted travel and, in some cases, it provided the information necessary for the Passport Office to refuse to issue a passport altogether.

The territorial restriction printed on many passports, including the British, was first introduced during the First

World War and like other restrictions whose imposition the public would never have accepted in peacetime, when that peace came, it was decided by those in power that, actually, the restriction might just as well stay in place. The League of Nations passport conference in Paris in 1920 compounded this state of affairs by initially accepting the territorial restriction as an integral characteristic of their recommended 'international passport'.

However, a sub-committee on the passport regime of the same League met in Paris five years later. It recommended that countries should issue passports 'valid for all countries'. A meeting was immediately called at the Foreign Office between interested heads of department. This included the Chief Passport Officer, Mr Martin; the Chief Inspector of the Immigration Branch of the Home Office, Mr Haldane Porter and the Chief Passport Control Officer, Major R. Spencer. The military rank of the latter is a clue to whom his real employer was; none other than the Director of Military Intelligence. The purpose of the meeting was to decide on a strategy on territorial restrictions in passports to present to the imminent 1926 Passport Conference in Geneva. The opinions expressed in the meeting are not those one would normally attribute to government departments committed to facilitating the travel of their own subjects without let or hindrance.

Mr Martin explained that if the practice of endorsing passports valid for a given destination were abolished, all controls would go by the board and he strongly maintained the view that the retention of the system was essential. Some of the reasons he submitted in support of his assertions may seem a little disingenuous nowadays: the Foreign Office was bound by its duties to Parliament to maintain a check on theatrical artistes who were susceptible to being lured into the White Slave Traffic by spurious contracts promoted by undesirable organisations. Another reason was that persons signing emigration papers for some

South American countries had no idea that the conditions awaiting them were unsuitable. By divulging their intended destination when applying for a passport they gave the Overseas Settlement Department the opportunity of warning them of the true situation. This view was endorsed by Mr Plant of the Overseas Development Office who proudly declared that as things stood, his department had been able to stop numerous emigrants from going to countries where there was no opening for them. This also saved public funds since, had they travelled, they would have become destitute and been repatriated at public expense. However, not all the chiefs saw their position as impregnable. Haldane Porter of the Immigration Branch suggested that the boat should not be rocked lest passports were done away with altogether.[10]

The fervent belief of the civil servants in the rectitude of their judgement, supported by the mores and opinions of the time enabled them to take decisions which nowadays would be considered as gross arrogance. Thus in July 1922, a passport was refused to Miss Elisabeth Pickford. She intended to travel out to Iraq as the secretary of a British Subject. He was known not only to have been a native of Baghdad who had been naturalised in the Straits Settlements, but also to be of 'bad character'. Similarly in July 1925, Miss Doris R Reeves was prevented from taking her claimed employment in Greece because it was known that she intended to live as mistress to a young Greek. No explanation was given of how they had learned this information.

Some unfortunate people had the ignominy of being refused passports not even on individual grounds but because they fell within a certain category, such as British Subjects travelling to New Zealand who were not of European race and did not possess the special permit issued by the New Zealand government. This category was evidence of the use by British colonial governments of the territorial restrictions facility on British passports to control selectively immigration to their own countries. The India Office observed that the system was essential for them; it was the only control they could exercise because they had no immigration laws.[11]

But apart from the fatherly protection of vulnerable females, the discouragement of idealist emigrants to South America and the insidious exclusion of non-Europeans from parts of the British Empire, what was the real reason for the government departments fighting to restrict the worldwide validity of its passports? It was a matter of intelligence gathering and surveillance of its own citizens.

The Military Intelligence Department, MI5, was usually referred to in official files as 'another department' or 'an interested department'; latterly it became identified by its Post Office box number: Box 500. Back in 1920, Mr Martin put forward perhaps the only genuine reason why MI5 wished to retain the territorial restrictions facility on passports. '...it was important for the various departments of His Majesty's Government to know the movements of certain individuals and this could only be achieved if they were forced when applying for a passport to declare their country of destination.'[12]

The idea that passports were there as tools of control had been sustained by the internal security services of many countries. For such organisations the actual legwork was usually undertaken by the local police – it was they who had to compile the registers and check the addresses. This working cooperation with the security service infused the police with a similar ethos, such that they also desired to control by passport. In 1929, at a conference in the Foreign Office of the heads of interested sections, one conclusion was: 'Passports should therefore be refused at the request of the Police, to any person known and to habitual criminals suspected, to be leaving this country for the purpose of committing crimes abroad or of organising abroad crimes to be committed in this country. On the other hand the mere fact that a man has been convicted of crime is not in itself a reason for refusal he may be anxious to make a new start in another country.'[13]

How reassuring it was that the delegates could recognise some redeeming characteristics in criminals! However, the absolutist root of the opinion persisted. At the 1947 session of the International Criminal Police Commission the delegates were unanimous in the draconian measure that any criminal convicted of a crime either of international character or with international ramifications should be excluded from holding a passport altogether.[14]

The deceit and duplicity exercised by government departments in refusing or withholding passports obliged them to adopt some convoluted positions. Thus when Mr Petrie of the Office of the High Commissioner for South Africa dropped in to the Foreign Office in September 1948 to enquire whether Great Britain had in the past refused passports to persons of doubtful ideological persuasions and if so, how had they done it? Mr Jay of the Foreign Office opined that: '...since this request comes from the present South African Government. The statement should, I think, be less full than might be prepared in a reply to a similar request had it emanated, say, from the Canadian Government.'[15] An interesting example of a government withholding information on ideological grounds about a government withholding passports for the same reason.

This desire to control citizens whilst lulling them into the belief that they were being facilitated was not an exclusive obsession of the British. The USA made foreign travel without a passport unlawful by section 215 of the US Immigration and Naturalisation Act 1952. It then prohibited its citizens from visiting certain countries and threatened them with prosecution if they managed it nevertheless. In 1955, to the list of countries to which American citizens were prohibited from travelling they added 'portions of China under Communist control'. The Chinese found this insulting and in 1957 denied entry anywhere in its territory to American journalists. By 1959, thirty-one had been refused access. This was a masterly move since journalists are a body of people who have the knowledge and power to exert influence on governments. The result was that the American consular officers were ordered to block out the offending words.

Perhaps the solution is to travel without a passport. Formerly, this was quite easy. In 1596, a German named Ludwig von Auhalt Cothen, travelled to England with his older brother, tutor and page. When they arrived off the port of Gravesend they were asked to show their passports. They had brought none with them but they managed to convince the officials that they were coming to visit universities; this purpose presumably appeared harmless

THIS PASSPORT IS NOT VALID FOR TRAVEL TO OR IN COMMUNIST CONTROLLED PORTIONS OF

CHINA
KOREA
VIET-NAM

OR TO OR IN

ALBANIA
CUBA

A PERSON WHO TRAVELS TO OR IN THE LISTED COUNTRIES OR AREAS MAY BE LIABLE FOR PROSECUTION UNDER SECTION 1185, TITLE 8, U.S. CODE, AND SECTION 1544, TITLE 18, U.S. CODE.

How to upset everybody. This endorsement by the American authorities in a USA passport of 1965 caused a political row with China and a civil liberties confrontation with its own citizens.

enough and they were allowed in.[16] Three centuries later, one of their compatriots was less fortunate. A German spy called Silber, gained employment in the British Postal Censorship Office during the First World War, the very office, incidentally, that was employed to check upon the letters of people such as Lody. He found that at the end of the war he was unable to return home. He had entered illegally in 1914 without documents and in 1919 Germany had no representatives in the UK who could issue him with a passport. He eventually had to await for the reopening of the no-passport excursions to Belgium in 1924 in order to be able to leave England without a passport.[17]

In some areas of the world there has recently been a subtle change in the purpose of frontier document checks. Whilst the agent inspecting the papers was an employee of the government, a person travelling without a passport for whatever reason – emergency, forgetfulness or even sheer cussedness – could be allowed to proceed because the official could make the decision in the full knowledge of the rules and regulations. With the levying by governments of financial penalties on airlines and shipping companies who carry incorrectly documented travellers, a thorough document check is now carried out by the employee of the carrying company. He knows that any exercise of discretion on his part to allow a traveller to board without a passport is likely to cost his company money.

Money is an important consideration when assessing the purpose of a passport. In the 1830s, a British passport cost £2 7s 6d (£2.37$^{1}/_{2}$). In the following twenty years it was reduced to 7s 6d (37$^{1}/_{2}$p), then 6s (30p) then finally in 1858, to 2s. (10p).

This train of reductions was brought about largely by public demand for cheaper passports or preferably, no passports at all. But it requires closer inspection, for although the price of a London-issued Foreign Office passport was 2s, if the British traveller applied at a consulate abroad for a passport, he was charged 5*s*. The reason for this was to generate an income for the Consul. Indeed many consuls complained to the Foreign Office in 1858 when the London fee was reduced to 2*s*, for travellers then preferred to purchase a cheaper Foreign Office passport before leaving the UK. In considering the maintenance of the consular passport fee in 1886, a Foreign Office official observed, '...the fee is 5/- [25p] and I anticipate a very welcome addition to our consular fees from this source.'[18]

In 1909, a British passport cost only 5p more than it had fifty years earlier. By the outbreak of the Second World War, the fee was 15*s* (75p) for a passport whose total validity was now ten years. The public was led to believe that, in accordance with the tenets of the League of Nations passport conference, the passport was a facility provided at cost by the government, the only income derived from it being a paltry duty stamp of 6*d* (2^1/$_2$p) which was paid to the Treasury.

This was, strictly speaking, quite truthful but it skirted around the wider issue that by maintaining a passport system, countries were able to insist upon visas. During the First World War the UK had posted Passport Control Officers to various consulates abroad to issue visas. When the war was over, the postings were maintained for 'security reasons'. The officers were paid between £800 and £1,000 p.a. depending upon their location and in 1921 they made a profit of £19,600 for the Foreign Office. The system was regularly bringing in profits in excess of £1,300 per month. Not all posts flourished, Rome for example lost £1,040 in 1921 and Prague £860 but with posts like Paris turning in an annual profit of £20,500, it was not in the Government's interest to abandon a passport and visa system which subsidised its Foreign Office to this extent. This view was endorsed by Lord William Percy who was charged with compiling a report on the running of the Passport Control Offices in Europe in 1921. He observed: '...in the absence of the Passport Control the Immigration Service would require augmentation, that increased expenditure would fall upon the British taxpayer, whereas the control abroad is not only paid for by the alien traveller but produces some tens of thousands of revenue...'[19]

The possibility that a passport system could be a revenue earner has long been known to the authorities, whether local or national. In 1641, John Evelyn, while travelling in the troubled Netherlands of the time, disembarked one day before the fort of Lillo, near Antwerp.

> Being taken before the Governor, he demanded my passe, to which he set his hand and asked two rix-dollars for a fee, which methought appeared very unhandsome in a Soldier of his quality. I told him that I had already purchased my passe of the Commissaries at Roterdam; at which, in a greate fury snatching the paper out of my hand, he flung it scornfully under a table and bad me try whether I could get to Antwerp without his permission...[20]

Should one be in any doubt as to whether passports were seen as a source of income for the government one only has to examine the financing of its departments. In 1932, a parliamentary private secretary by the name of Anthony Eden explained to the House of Commons why the government was asking for a supplementary sum of up to £1,500 to pay for the running of the Foreign Office. When making the estimate in the previous year they had counted upon the income to be received from issuing passports. Unfortunately this had fallen short of expectations because the government had asked the public in view of the economic situation, to holiday at home and they had done so. This had created a shortfall in passport issues: '...due to the patriotism of the British public in refraining from travelling abroad in a time of national need...'[21] The government's immediate response, of course, was to double the fee for a passport from 7s 6d (37½p) to 15s (75p).

During the Revolutionary period in France, the increase in the number of identity documents which was deemed necessary was seen as a boon by town Mayors who would insist upon affixing their seal and charging a fee. The first thing that the US Department of State did when it decreed that henceforth it should have the monopoly for issuing passports, was to make applicants pay for them. At the League of Nations Conference, Bulgaria openly declared that it needed to make money from issuing passports because it was nearly bankrupt. Up to the end of 1923, 0.22% of the war reparation receipts paid to the Allied Powers under the terms of the Treaty of Versailles was represented by the revenue obtained from issuing the identity permits and other passes which were demanded of people wishing to move in and out of Germany.[22] In its trading year of 2000–1, from each adult passport fee it received, the United Kingdom Passport Service gave over £8 (more than £29m in total) to the Foreign & Commonwealth Office to cover the costs incurred by the latter in providing passports and consular services to travellers overseas.[23] It would be naive to imagine any government willing to abolish such a revenue-earning passport system.

In the nineteenth century the most important function of a passport was to impress foreigners. To achieve this it employed elaborate crests and flowery writing, wax seals and intricate embossing stamps. It was bluff and bluster – look how important my country is! The physical identification of the holder seemed to be of secondary importance. As the purpose of the passport began to evolve so did its construction and design. Today's passport impresses one most by its attempt to infallibly identify the holder and by its utter failure to maintain its country's standing. Comparing the quality of any present-day passport with that of one issued 150 years earlier shows a disparity quite detrimental to our time.

Benjamin Franklin, the USA's innovative minister plenipotentiary in Paris who designed and printed some of the first American republican passports, figured in a passport design himself two centuries later when, in April 1993, the USA introduced its new anti-fraud passport. This had a green fabric cover in place of the former blue card cover, specially designed pages to foil forgers and a kinegram affixed across the corner of the photograph. It was on this device, which was similar to a hologram, that the head of Benjamin Franklin could be found. Six weeks after its introduction a member of IATA claimed in a trade publication that the passport was less secure than the one it had replaced for the laminate and kinegram could be peeled back and the holder's details changed. The Department of State stood resolutely by its passport... for almost a year. In April 1994 it introduced an improved, blue cover version which incorporated 'additional security features'.

In passport control, the tail is wagging the dog. The process of assessing the traveller is being dictated by the document. Entire conceptions have had to be discarded. A passport-control officer voicing the opinion of the nineteenth-century British Consul in Le Havre that 'I found his appearance was not that of an Englishman' would today find himself before a disciplinary board on racial discrimination grounds.[24]

Today, passports are studded with holograms and lathered with print that changes colour; they talk to machines and interfere with colour photocopiers and yet they are still misused. When the officer's suspicions are aroused he now uses the quick, irrefutable technical checks at his disposal. He flips the passport under the UV light – the designs fluoresce in all the right places; he holds it obliquely to the window – the latent image in the intaglio printing surges into view; he peers through his filters – the inks change colours where they should. Three times convinced of the genuineness of the passport, he glances at the photograph. The man before him is an imposter who has shaved his eyebrows to match those on the photograph, grown a moustache and restyled his hair. It is impossible to determine for certain whether or not it is the same person because the photograph is now a highly secure but low-definition digital image. It cannot be peeled from the page but it does not have the quality of the studio photographs of eighty years earlier. A queue is building up before the officer's desk. His management now work to performance targets and customer satisfaction surveys. His pay is linked to the results. What do you think he does?

What is the future for the passport? It has survived centuries because of two factors – it is a concept that is adaptable and there have been persistent demands upon it to adapt. Whether the need arises for it to continue adapting in the twenty-first century will depend on the evolution of interstate relations and the security demands of individual states. Already, in Europe, the facilitation quality of the passport is no longer needed. Nationals of the European Area can travel freely throughout more than a dozen countries – this has been negotiated at suprastate level. The passport is just a document proving membership of the club.

Physically reflecting the idea of club membership is the development of the plastic card passport, first discussed as far back as the 1970s. It continues the downward progress in size from the large single sheet, through the double sheet, the sheet folded into covers, the hard-covered booklet, the smaller hard-covered booklet and the small soft-covered booklet. Because of technical advances in data storage, the plastic card passport can carry far more information than its ancestors, so why restrict it to a travel card? Why not make it a social-security, health, employment and identity card? When the German EC passport was introduced it was thought necessary to append to its plastic identity card a passport booklet to allow countries a space for visas. How long will it be before somebody realises that all the endorsements can be made electronically on a central database as the card is swiped through the control point?

And yet, the pressure to produce a plastic data-card type passport has nothing to do with travelling; it is concerned with control. Once you have a plastic passport, a credit card and a mobile phone, the government will know twenty-four hours a day who you are, where you are, what you are doing, and how much it is costing you. (And who you are doing it with as well.)

Is the passport a restriction or a facility, a munificence or a revenue earner, a weapon of control or a tool of freedom? The colour of the answer, rather like the hologram on the passport, depends upon which angle you look at it from. There is no doubt that as long as passports are required for travel, governments will lie about them; fraudsters and terrorists will misuse them and innocent travellers will be inconvenienced by them.

What does the traveller get for his money? A cheapskate booklet costing a few pence to manufacture, hopefully issued in the correct identity by an organisation which would not know if it were not. It purports to allow you to pass without let or hindrance but in international law, a passport has no standing. One country cannot, by unilaterally issuing a document, oblige another to comply with its wishes. Only the safe conduct issued in time of war by a belligerent to allow a diplomat to leave enemy territory, is recognised internationally as having legal force. In the United Kingdom, you are not even entitled as of right to a passport; it is a royal prerogative, against the refusal of which, there is no appeal.

Passports have been saviours of lives and executioners; the path to freedom and the prison bars; guarantees of prosperity and harbingers of impoverishment. They have been brandished across borders with jingoistic taunts, they have been treated with deference and obsequiousness, they have been insulted and defaced in the course of their duty. Through all this, they have somehow always managed to reflect a core element of their time; whether it was the pragmatic romanticism of the Victorians in their printed cursive script or the contemporary obsession with human self-effacement as evidenced by the current desire to teach machines to do poorly what a human can do so well.

And despite and because of all their qualities and faults, you know... I rather like passports.

NOTES

Chapter One
1. Wallis J.E.P. *Reports of State Trials New Series* (HMSO, 1898) Vol. VIII.
2. Hansard *Parliamentary Debates* 5.2.1858.
3. Ibid.
4. HMSO *Select Committee on Consular Service and Appointments. Minutes of Evidence* (1858).
5. *The Times* 4.2.1858.
6. Lord Palmerston, *Hansard* 8.2.1858.
7. Ibid.
8. Mr Roebuck, MP for Sheffield in *Hansard* (8.2.1858).
9. Mr Gilpin, MP for Northampton in *Hansard* (8.2.1858).
10. *Hansard* 23.3.1858.

Chapter Two
1. W.S. Lewis *Horace Walpole's Correspondence with Sir Horace Mann* (OUP, 1960).
2. 2 Ed. VI c.2.
3. Sir J. Gardner Wilkinson *A Popular Account of the Ancient Egyptians, Their Life and Customs* (John Murray, 1854).
4. Nehemiah 2: 7-9
5. C.A.J. Skeel *Travel in the 1st Century after Christ* (CUP 1901).
6. G.N. Garmonsway *The Anglo Saxon Chronicle* (Dent, 1953).
7. T.W.E.Roche *The Key in the Lock* (John Murray, 1969).
8. J. Fairburn *Fairburn's Edition of Magna Charta* (1810).
9. Ibid.
10. B. Vincent *Haydn's Dictionary of Dates* (Bowden & Co,1892).

Chapter Three
1. G. Home *Old London Bridge* (Bodley Head, 1931).
2. K. Van Loewe *The Lithuanian Statute of 1529* (E.J.Brill, 1976).
3. Ibid
4. F.A.Mumby *Elizabeth and Mary Stuart* (*Constable & Co,* 1914).
5. Ibid.
6. Ibid

7. Ibid
8. Sir H. Ellis *Original Letters Illustrative of English History* (Richard Bentley, 1836), Vol. III.
9. W.D. Rohan Scott *German Travellers in England 1400–1800* (Blackwell, 1953).
10. Ibid
11. W. Foster *The Journal of John Jourdain 1600–1617* (Hakluyt Society, 1905).
12. US Passport Office *The United States Passport* (Department of State Publications, 1976).
13. J. Parkes *Travel in England in the Seventeenth Century* (OUP, 1925).

Chapter Four
1. A. Sée *Le Passeport en France* (Faculté de Droit, 1907).
2. W. S. Lewis & A. D. Wallace *Horace Walpole's Correspondences with Mary and Agnes Berry and Barbara Cecilia Seton* (Yale University Press, 1944).
3. W. Wickham *The Correspondence of the Right Honourable William Wickham* (Richard Bentley, 1870).
4. Baronne de Stael *Dix Années d'Exil* (Treuttel & Wurtz, 1821).
5. C. Colvin *Maria Edgeworth in France and Switzerland* (Clarendon Press, 1974).
6. US Passport Office *The United States Passport* (Department of State Publications, 1976).
7. 33 Geo. III c. 4.
8. F. Galton *Vacation Tourists and Notes of Travel in 1860* (Macmillan & Co., 1861).
9. J. Forster *The Life of Charles Dickens* (Chapman & Hall, 1870)
10. J. Gadsby *My Wanderings Being Travels in the East* (Gadsby, 1883).
11. Ibid.
12. Ibid.
13. Ibid.
14. Ibid.
15. Ibid.
16. J. Foster Fraser *Round the World on a Wheel* (Nelson & Sons, 1899).

17. Ibid.
18. John Murray *Japan* (John Murray, 1894).

Chapter Five
1. *The Times* (31.10.1914).
2. *The Times* (1.11.1914).
3. *The New York Times* (25.11.1914).
4. *The Times* (26.2.1853).
5. *Punch* (18.4.1863).
6. Passport Office application form 1920.
7. Passport Office application form 1940.
8. US Passport Office *The United States Passport* (Department of State Publications, 1976).
9. Public Record Office file, FO 612/201.
10. *The Times* (28.2.1957).
11. T. Geoffrey *An Immigrant in Japan* (T. Werner Laurie Ltd., 1926).

Chapter Six
1. PRO file, FO 614/2.
2. Ibid.
3. Ibid.
4. Ibid.
5. PRO file, FO 366/791.
6. League of Nations *Replies from Governments to the Enquiry on the Application of the Recommendations of the Passport Conference of 1926* (Geneva, 1937).
7. Ibid.
8. Ibid.
9. Ibid.
10. Ibid
11. PRO file, FO 612/355.
12. League of Nations *Replies from Governments.*

Chapter Seven
1. Foreign Office notice dated 21.4.1858.
2. PRO file, FO 612/209.
3. PRO file, FO 612/356.
4. Ibid.
5. Ibid.

6. Ibid.
7. Ibid.
8. Ibid.
9. PRO file, FO 612/290.
10. European Communities Bulletin 7/75 *Towards European Citizenship* (1975).

Chapter Eight
1. J.W. Hall *The Trial of William Joyce* (Butterwoth & Co.,1946).
2. J.P.V.D. Balsdon *Romans and Aliens* (Duckworth, 1979).
3. F. Rasoloniaina *Recueil des Textes Legislatifs et Reglementaires Malgaches* (CMPL, 1983).
4. H.Y. Jung *Double Citizenship in Malaysia* (Nanyang University, 1974).
5. H. Crouch *A Complete View of the British Customs* (Osborn & Longman, 1731).
6. J.D. Whelpley *The Problem of the Immigrant* (Chapman & Hall, 1905).
7. Home Office *Handbook on the Peculiarities of Foreign Names* (1950).

Chapter Nine
1. J. W. Gerard *My Four Years in Germany* (Hodder & Stoughton, 1917.
2. Information related to author by source wishing to remain anonymous.
3. PRO file, FO 612/357.
4. R. Dimbleby *The Frontiers are Green* (Hodder & Stoughton, 1945).

Chapter Ten
1. *The Times* (various 1922).
2. W. Bray (ed.), *The Diary of John Evelyn* (W. W. Gibbings, 1890).
3. US Passport Office *The United States Passport* (Department of State Publications, 1976).
4. C. Smith *Carlos, Portrait of a Terrorist* (Mandarin, 1995).
5. *The Times* (17.1.2002).
6. HMSO *Select Committee on Consular Service and Appointments.* (1858).

7.   P. Lowe *Counterfeiting in China* (Inernational Chamber of Commerce, 1995).

8.   R. Lemkin *L'Unification des Incriminations en Matière de Falsification des Passeports et Déclarations d'Identité* (Imprimerie Nationale, 1938).

9.   H. B. Gisevius *To The Bitter End* (Cape, 1948).

10. W. Wickham *The Correspondence of the Right Honourable William Wickham* (Richard Bentley, 1870).

Chapter Eleven

1.   *The Times* (27.5.1791).

2.   E. d'Hauterive *Journal of the Comte d'Espinchal* (Chapman & Hall, 1912).

3.   *The Times (*28.7.1851)

4   E. Hambloch *British Consul* (Harrap & Co., 1938).

5.   *Daily Telegraph* (16.2.2002).

6.   PRO file ST14/3809

7.   A. Seé *Le Passeport en France* (Faculté de Droit, 1907).

8.   Ibid.

9.   *The Times* (17.2.1915).

10. PRO file, FO 612/355.

11. Ibid

12. Ibid

13. PRO file, FO 612/273

14. PRO file, FO 612/356

15. PRO file, FO 612/273

16. W.D.Rohan Scott *German Travellers in England 1400–1800* (Blackwell, 1953).

17. J.C. Silber *Les Armes Invisibles* (Payot, 1933).

18. PRO file, FO 614/1

19. PRO file, FO 366/794

20   W. Bray (ed.), *The Diary of John Evelyn* (W. W. Gibbings, 1890).

21. *Hansard* 9.3.1932

22. L'Imprimerie de l'Armeé du Rhin *Un An d'Occupation* (1924).

23. United Kingdom Passport Service *Annual Report and Accounts 2000–2001* (The Stationery Office, 2001).

24. HMSO, *Select Committee on Consular Service and Appointments.* (1858).

BIBLIOGRAPHY

Primary Sources - Files in the Public Record Office
In the Foreign Office files, Passport Office sub series, prefix FO:

366/545, 366/791, 366/794, 366/802, 366/815, 366/825,
612/108, 612/182, 612/198, 612/201, 612/209, 612/226,
612/273, 612/280, 612/282, 612/290, 612/298, 612/334,
612/354, 612/355, 612/356, 612/357, 612/358, 614/1,
614/2.

In the Stationery Office series, prefix STAT:
12/37/10, 12/54, 12/139/17, 14/1166, 14/1417, 14/1428
14/3809

Secondary Sources

Books
Place of publication is London unless stated.

Baedeker, K. *Palestine and Syria,* Leipzig, 1876
Balsdon, J.P.V.D. *Romans and Aliens,* Duckworth, 1979
Bell, G.K.A. *Humanity and the Refugees,* The Jewish Historical
 Society of England, 1939
Benians, E.A. *Race and Nation in the United States,* CUP, 1946
Binmore, C.J. *The Canadian Nationality,* Hamilton Adams & Co,
 1888
Borrie, W.D. *Immigration – Australia's problems and prospects,* Angus
 & Robertson, Sydney, 1949
Bray, W. (ed.), *The Diary of John Evelyn,* W.W.Gibbings, 1890
Brookes, R. *The General Gazeteer,* 1812
Bury, J.T.P. (ed.), *The Zenith of European War,* CUP, 1971
Campbell, Revd. W. (ed.), *Chronicles and Memorials of Great Britain
 and Ireland During the Middle Ages,* Longman & Co, 1873 Vol 1,
 (Henry VII).
Carter Gilmour, S. *Paper, Its Making, Merchanting and Usage,*
 Longmans, Green & Co, 1955
Chambers, R.W. *England Before the Norman Conquest,* Longmans,
 Green & Co, 1926

Clunn, H. *The Face of Paris*, Simpkin Marshall, 1933

Cobb, R.C. *The Police and the People*, Oxford, OUP, 1970

Colvin, C. (ed.), *Maria Edgeworth in France and Switzerland*, Oxford, Clarendon Press, 1974

Crawley, C.W. (ed.), *War and Peace in an Age of Upheaval 1793-1830*, CUP, 1969

Crouch, H. *A Complete View of the British Customs*, Osborn & Longman, 1731

Cunningham, W. *Alien Immigrants to England*, George Allen & Unwin, 1897

Curner Briggs, N. & Gambier, R. *Huguenot Ancestry*, Phillimore, 1985

Dardy, C. *Identités de Papier*, Lieu Commun, 1990

Dimbleby, R. *The Frontiers are Green*, Hodder and Stoughton, 1945

Dumont, E. *Recollections of Mirabeau and of the two first Legislative Assemblies of France*, Edward Bull, 1832

East, W. G. & Moodie, A. E. *The Changing World*, Harrap, 1956

Elias, Dr. T. O. *The British Commonwealth – The Development of its Law and Constitutions*, Stevens & Sons, 1967, Vol 14

Ellis, Sir H. (ed.), *Original Letters Illustrative of English History*, Richard Bentley, 1836 Vol III

Eppstein, J. *Ten Years' Life of the League of Nations*, The May Fair Press, 1929

Evans, R.J. *The Victorian Age 1815-1914*, Edward Arnold, 1950

Fairburn, J. *Fairburn's Edition of Magna Charta*, 1810

Farndale, N. *Haw-Haw. The Tragedy of William and Margaret Joyce* Macmillan, 2005

Forster, J. *The Life of Charles Dickens*, Chapman & Hill, 1870

Foster Fraser, J. *Round the World on a Wheel*, Nelson & Sons, 1899

Foster, W. (ed.), *The Journal of John Jourdain 1608-1617*, Cambridge, Hakluyt Society, 1905

Fouché, J. *Mémoires de Joseph Fouché, Duc d'Otrante*, Paris, Le Rouge, 1824

Gadsby, J. *My Wanderings being Travels in the East*, Gadsby, 1883

Galignani *New Paris Guide*, Paris, A. & W. Galignani, 1848

Galton, F. (ed.), *Vacation Tourists and Notes of Travel in 1860*, Macmillan and Co, 1861.

Gardner Wilkinson, Sir J. *A Popular Account of the Ancient Egyptians*, J. Murray, 1854

Garmonsway, G.N. *The Anglo Saxon Chronicle*, Dent, 1953

Geoffrey, T. *An Immigrant in Japan,* T. Werner Laurie Ltd, 1926

Gerard, J.W. *My Four Years in Germany,* Hodder & Stoughton, 1917

Gernsheim, H. *The History of Photography,* OUP, 1955

Gisevius, H.B. *To The Bitter End,* Cape, 1948

Gordon, P. *Passport Raids and Checks,* Runnymede Trust, 1981

Griffiths, A. *Mysteries of Police and Crime,* Cassell, 1903

Guyot, A. *Almanach Impérial,* Paris, Guyot et Scribe, 1856

Hall, J.W. *The Trial of William Joyce,* Butterworth & Co., 1946

Hambloch, E. *British Consul,* Harrap & Co, 1938

Hanford, J.H. *John Milton, Englishman,* New York, Crown, 1949

Hansard *Parliamentary Debates,* C. Buck, 1858, Vol CXLVIII

d'Hauterive, E. *Journal of the Comte d'Espinchal,* Chapman & Hall, 1912

Henriques, H.S.Q. *Law of Aliens & Naturalization,* Butterworth & Co, 1906

Hill, M.C. *The King's Messengers 1199-1377,* Arnold, 1961

Home, G. *Old London Bridge,* Bodley Head, 1931

Home Office. *Handbook on the Peculiarities of Foreign Names,* 1950

Humphrey, D. & Ward M. *Passports and Politics,* Penguin, 1974

Hynd, A. *Passport to Treason,* New York, Mc.Bride & Co, 1944

L'Imprimerie de l'Armée du Rhin. *Un An d'Occupation,* Dusseldorf, 1924

Jones, J.M. *British Nationality Law and Practice,* Oxford, Clarendon Press, 1947

Jung, H. Y. *Double Citizenship in Malaysia,* Singapore, Nanyang University, 1970

Kershaw, R. & Pearsall, M. *Immigrants and Aliens,* Richmond, Public Record Office, 2000

Knapp, V. (ed.), *International Encyclopaedia of Comparative Law,* Tubingen, J.C.B. Mohr, 1993

Lemkin, R. *L'Unification des Incriminations en Matière de Falsification des Passeports et Déclarations d'Identité,* Cairo, Imprimerie Nationale, 1938

Lewis, Sir G. C. *On the Government of Dependencies,* Oxford, Clarendon Press, 1890

Lewis, W. S. & Wallace, A. D. (ed.), *Horace Walpole's Correspondences with Mary and Agnes Berry and Barbara Cecilia Seton,* Yale University Press, 1944

Lewis, W.S. (ed.), *Horace Walpole's Correspondence with Sir Horace Mann,* OUP, 1960

Loewe, K.Van (tr.), *The Lithuanian Statute of 1529*, Leiden, E. J. Brill, 1976

Lowe, P. *Counterfeiting in China*, Barking, International Chamber of Commerce, 1995

Macartney, C.A. *Refugees*, League of Nations, 1929

Machiavelli *The Prince*, George Routledge & Sons, 1883

Mackenzie, C. *My Life and Times*, Chatto & Windus, 1966, Vol V

Mackie, J.D. *The Earlier Tudors 1485-1558*, Oxford, Clarendon Press, 1952

Montmorin, A. M. de *Monsieur de Montmorin Accusé*, Paris, l'Imprimerie de Chaudriet, 1791

Mumby, F.A. *Elizabeth and Mary Stuart*, Constable and Co, 1914

Murray, J. *Japan*, Edinburgh, John Murray, 1894

Nicholson, C. *Strangers to England*, Wayland, 1974

Niemeyer, T. and Strupp, K *Jahrbuch des Volkerrechts*, Leipzig, Dancker & Humblot, 1914

Page, W. *Letters of Denization and Acts of Naturalization for Aliens in England 1509-1603*, The Huguenot Society, 1893

Parkes, J. *Travel in England in the Seventeenth Century*, OUP, 1925

Purchas, S. *Hakluytus Posthumus*, Glasgow, James MacLehose, 1905

Rasoloniaina, F. *Recueil des Textes Legislatifs et Reglementaires Malgaches*, Madagascar, CMPL, 1983

Roche, T.W.E. *The Key in the Lock*, John Murray, 1969

Rohan Scott, W. D. *German Travellers in England 1400-1800*, Oxford, Blackwell, 1953

Royal Institute of International Affairs. *The Status of Aliens in China*, 1931

Rye, W. B. *England as Seen by Foreigners in the Days of Elizabeth and James the First*, New York, Benjamin Blom, 1967

St.J Packe, M. *Orsini The Story of a Conspirator*, Boston, Little Brown & Co, 1957

Sée, A. *Le Passeport en France*, Faculté de Droit, Université de Paris, 1907

Shaw, W.A. *Letters of Denization and Acts of Naturalization for Aliens in England 1603-1800*, The Huguenot Society, 1911

Silber, J. C. *Les Armes Invisibles*, Paris, Payot, 1933

Skeel, C.A.J. *Travel in the 1st Century after Christ*, Cambridge, CUP, 1901

Smith, A.D. *National Identity*, Penguin, 1991

Smith, C. *Carlos Portrait of a Terrorist,* Mandarin, 1995

Stael, Baronne de. *Dix Années d'Exil,* Paris, Treuttel & Wurtz, 1821

Sterne, L. *A Sentimental Journey,* New York, William Belasco & Meyers, 1930

Stuart, G.H. and Whitton, J.B.. *Conception Américaine des Relations Internationales,* Publications de la Conciliation Internationale, Paris, 1935

Suttaby, R. & A. *The Royal Kalendar and Court and City Register for England, Scotland, Ireland and the Colonies,* 1859

Torpey, J. *The Invention of the Passport. Surveillance, Citizen and the State,* Cambridge CUP, 2000

Trill, H.D. and Mann J.S. (eds.), *Social England,* Cassell & Co, 1901, Vol. 1

Twiss, Sir T. (ed.) *The Black Book of the Admiralty,* Longman & Co, 1871

The United States Passport Office. *The United States Passport,* Washington, Department of State Publications, 1976

Vincent, B. *Haydn's Dictionary of Dates,* Ward Lock, Bowden & Co, 1892

Vincent, H. *Newfoundland to Cochin China,* Sampson Low, Marston & Co, 1892

Wallis, J.E.P. (ed.), *Reports of State Trials, New Series* HMSO, 1898, Vol VIII

Webb, K. *Refugees 1960,* Penguin, 1960

West, R. *The Meaning of Treason,* Macmillan & Co, 1952

Wheeler-Holohan, V. *The History of the King's Messengers,* Grayson & Grayson, 1935

Whelpley, J.D. *The Problem of the Immigrant,* Chapman & Hall, 1905

Wickham, W. *The Correspondence of the Right Honourable William Wickham,* Richard Bentley, 1870

Wicks, M.C.W. *The Italian Exiles in London 1814-1848,* New York, Books for Libraries Press, 1968

Wilson, T. & Donnen, H. *Border Identities, Nation and State at International Frontiers,* CUP, 1998

Newspapers, Official Reports and Other Publications.

Anonymous, 'Soviet Work Books and the Internal Passport System', circa 1952

Connor, S. 'The Invisible Border Guard,' *New Scientist,* 5.1.1984.

Deak, F. & Jessup, P.C. 'Prize Law Procedure at Sea – its Early

Development,' *The Tulane Law Review,* New Orleans, Tulane University of Louisiana, 1933, vol VII

Diplock, K. 'Passports and Protection in International Law', *The Grotius Society Transactions,* Wildy & Sons, 1946, Vol 32

European Communities Bulletin, 7/75 *Towards European Citizenship,* 1975

HMSO. *Select Committee on Consular Service and Appointments,* 1858

HMSO. *Report on the Manuscripts of Lady Du Cane,* 1905

HMSO. *The British Nationality and Status of Aliens Act (1914),* 1933

HMSO. *Convention Relating to the Status of Stateless Persons,* 1960

Home Office *Immigration, Nationality and Passports,* 1988

League of Nations. *Replies from Governments to the Enquiry on the Application of the Recommendations of the Passport Conference of 1926,* Geneva, 1937

The New York Times, various, 1919-93

Punch, 18.6.1863

The Times, various, 1790-2001.

United Kingdom Passport Service. *Annual Report and Accounts 2000-2001,* The Stationery Office, 2001

INDEX

Index

MARTIN LLOYD

The Trouble with France

Martin Lloyd's new international number one blockbusting bestseller

"...makes Baedeker's look like a guidebook..."

When Martin Lloyd set out on his holiday to Suffolk why did he end up in Boulogne? What caused Max the Mad Alsatian to steal his map and what did the knitted grandma really think of his display of hot plate juggling? The answers to these and many more mysteries are to be found in THE TROUBLE WITH FRANCE

THE TROUBLE WITH FRANCE contains no recipes and no hand drawn maps. It does not recount how somebody richer than you went to a part of France that you have never heard of, bought a stone ruin for a song and converted it into a luxurious retreat which they expect you to finance by buying their book.

Nor is it the self satisfied account of another ultra fit expedition cyclist abseiling down Everest on a penny farthing but Martin Lloyd attempting an uneventful ride on a mundane bicycle through an uninteresting part of France... and failing with outstanding success.

THE TROUBLE WITH FRANCE is destined to be a worldwide success now that Margaret's Mum has been down the road and told her friend Pat about it.

Published by Queen Anne's Fan ISBN: 9780 9547 15007

Martin Lloyd has recorded THE TROUBLE WITH FRANCE as a talking book for the blind. RNIB catalogue no: TB 15323

The Trouble with Spain

MARTIN LLOYD

FROM THE BESTSELLING AUTHOR OF
THE TROUBLE WITH FRANCE *COMES*
THIS EAGERLY AWAITED SEQUEL

"...makes Munchausen look like a liar..."

Still smarting from his brutal encounter with Gaul as detailed in his much acclaimed book, THE TROUBLE WITH FRANCE, Martin Lloyd drags his bicycle over the Pyrenees to pursue the twin delights of sun and breakfast.

What factor will defeat his proposed headlong plunge into raw hedonism? Will it be his profound and extensive ignorance of Spanish history or perhaps his coarse insensitivity to the culture of the peninsula?
Or would it be the damning condemnation that he is just too lazy to learn the language?

Read THE TROUBLE WITH SPAIN and you will discover nothing about bull fights and enjoy no colourful descriptions of sensual flamenco dancing but you will learn why you cannot train goldfish to be guard dogs and you will clearly understand why even Martin Lloyd's trousers ran away from him.

CAUTION
This book contains moderate use of humour, some expressions in foreign language and a short but ultimately frustrating scene in a lady's bedroom.

Published by Queen Anne's Fan ISBN: 9780 9547 15014

Hunting
the
Golden Lion

a cycle safari through France

Having recklessly declared in a previous book that it
must be possible to cross all of France staying only
in hotels called the HOTEL DU LION D'OR,
Martin Lloyd is challenged by his critics to prove
his assertion in the only way possible – by doing it.

Surely it will be a straightforward and leisurely ride
through France? As long as the hotels are no more than
a day's cycle ride apart, of course. And if your bicycle
has been constructed this century, and if you remember
to take with you all that you need... and if your name isn't
Martin Lloyd.

Is this why, on the the first day of his safari,
he is standing in his pyjamas on a pavement
a thousand miles from home,
clutching a broken bicycle
with a bleeding hand?

Published by Queen Anne's Fan ISBN: 9780 9547 1506 9

The
Chinese
Transfer

Martin Lloyd

The

Chinese Transfer

a thriller romance that you will
not want to put down

"...this is storytelling as it used to be..."

Paris in the 1970s – student demonstrations, union
strikes and oppressive heat. Coach driver Simon
Laperche is sent to Orly Airport to pick up a Chinese
group and take them to their hotel in the city. A run
of the mill job. He could do it with his eyes shut.
It was a pity about the guide, but then, he could
not expect to please everybody.

Abruptly, things go wrong. The plane is diverted to
Lyons and Laperche is ordered to drive his coach
south to meet it... and he has to take that infuriating
guide with him. Unknown to them both,
a terrorist unit has targeted their group and
is intent upon its destruction.

Stalked by the terrorists, the driver and guide continue
to bicker as they struggle to bring their group safely to
Paris. Will the mutual respect which eventually begins
to grow between them prove strong enough
when the test comes?

Published by Queen Anne's Fan ISBN: 9780 9547 15021

Rue Amélie

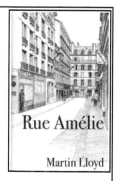

Rue Amélie

Martin Lloyd

another fast-paced thriller from Martin Lloyd.

Following the success of *The Chinese Transfer,* Martin Lloyd takes us back to the seedy side of Paris in the 1970s. Joel LeBatard, a driver for a small-time crook, loses his boss's car and his position. With no job and soon to be thrown out of his bedsit, he accepts a commission from a woman he meets at a funeral, to find out where her father had invested his secret pension.

LeBatard discovers that others are on the same trail – a ruthless big-time gangster whom he has already been stupid enough to upset, and an ex-colleague from his army days who now heads an undercover squad in the Ministry of Defence. They will stop at nothing to get their hands on the very thing that he is looking for, but nobody can tell him what it is.

The hectic action takes them to the four corners of Paris. Whilst pursuing his relentless search, LeBatard struggles with two difficulties: is his new employer telling him the truth and how, in the face of such energy and charm, can he uphold his vow never to get mixed up with another woman?

Published by Queen Anne's Fan ISBN: 9780 9547 1507 6

Every Picture

"... a tender and engaging love story..."

When Jennifer Pye bumped into Richard Ennessy on his first day at art college she did not know that he was a viscount and he did not tell her. Why should he? How was he to know that their paths would cross and recross and that he would end up falling in love with her?

And once that had happened, he then found it impossible to tell her the truth for fear of losing her. At the very moment that they finally admit their feelings for one another, the relationship is abruptly wrenched asunder as their lives take a violent and unpredictable turn, casting their two destinies onto divergent courses.

Would they ever meet again?

Published by Queen Anne's Fan ISBN: 9780 9547 1505 2